CoursePrep ExamGuide/StudyGuide MCSE Exam 70-270

Installing, Configuring, and Administering Microsoft Windows XP Professional

Australia • Canada • Mexico • Singapore • Spain • United Kingdom • United States

CoursePrep StudyGuide and *CoursePrep ExamGuide*
are published by Course Technology.

Associate Publisher
Steve Elliot

Product Manager
Charles Blum

Production Editor
Danielle Power

Developmental Editor
Jim Markham

Associate Product Manager
Tim Gleeson

Editorial Assistant
Nick Lombardi

Marketing Manager
Jason Sakos

Text Designer
GEX Publishing Services

Cover Designer
Betsy Young and
Abby Scholz

COPYRIGHT © 2002 Course Technology, a division of Thomson Learning, Inc. Thomson Learning™ is a trademark used herein under license.

Printed in Canada

1 2 3 4 5 WC 05 04 03 02

For more information, contact Course Technology, 25 Thomson Place, Boston, Massachusetts, 02210.

Or find us on the World Wide Web at: www.course.com

ALL RIGHTS RESERVED. No part of this work covered by the copyright hereon may be reproduced or used in any form or by any means—graphic, electronic, or mechanical, including photocopying, recording, taping, Web distribution, or information storage and retrieval systems—without the written permission of the publisher.

For permission to use material from this text or product, contact us by
Tel (800) 730-2214
Fax (800) 730-2215
www.thomsonrights.com

Microsoft and Windows are registered trademarks.

Disclaimer
Course Technology reserves the right to revise this publication and make changes from time to time in its content without notice.

ISBN 0-619-12032-0
ISBN 0-619-12119-X

TABLE OF CONTENTS

PREFACE vi

SECTION 1 INSTALLING WINDOWS XP PROFESSIONAL 1
    1.1 Perform an attended installation of Windows XP Professional.. 2
    1.2 Perform an unattended installation of Windows XP Professional.. 4
    1.2.1 Install Windows XP Professional by using Remote Installation Services (RIS).................... 6
    1.2.2 Install Windows XP Professional by using the System Preparation Tool 8
    1.2.3 Create unattended answer files by using Setup Manager to automate the installation
          of Windows XP Professional 10
    1.3 Upgrade from a previous version of Windows to Windows XP Professional..................... 12
    1.3.1 Prepare a computer to meet upgrade requirements.. 14
    1.3.2 Migrate existing user environments to a new installation 16
    1.4 Perform post-installation updates and product activation.. 18
    1.5 Troubleshoot failed installations 20

**SECTION 2 IMPLEMENTING AND CONDUCTING ADMINISTRATION
OF RESOURCES** 23
    2.1 Monitor, manage, and troubleshoot access to files and folders 24
    2.1.1 Configure, manage, and troubleshoot file compression 26
    2.1.2 Control access to files and folders by using permissions 28
    2.1.3 Optimize access to files and folders 30
    2.2 Manage and troubleshoot access to shared folders; create and remove shared folders;
         control access to shared folders by using permissions 32
    2.2.1 Manage and troubleshoot Web server resources... 34
    2.3 Connect to local and network print devices; connect to a local print device...................... 36
    2.3.1 Manage printers and print jobs 38
    2.3.2 Control access to printers by using permissions 40
    2.3.3 Connecting to an Internet printer 42
    2.4 Configure and manage file systems; convert from one file system to another
         file system; configure NTFS, FAT32, or FAT file systems... 44
    2.5 Manage and troubleshoot access to and synchronization of offline files........................... 46
    2.6 Configure and troubleshoot fax support 48

SECTION 3 IMPLEMENTING, MANAGING, MONITORING, AND TROUBLESHOOTING HARDWARE DEVICES AND DRIVERS ... 51

3.1 Implement, manage, and troubleshoot disk devices; monitor and configure disks; monitor, configure, and troubleshoot volumes ... 52

3.1.1 Install, configure, and manage DVD and CD-ROM devices ... 54

3.1.2 Monitor and configure removable media, such as tape devices ... 56

3.2 Implement, manage, and troubleshoot display devices; install, configure, and troubleshoot a video adapter ... 58

3.2.1 Configure multiple-display support ... 60

3.3 Configure Advanced Configuration Power Interface (ACPI) ... 62

3.4.1 Implement, manage, and troubleshoot input and output (I/O) devices; monitor, configure, and troubleshoot I/O devices, such as printers, scanners, multimedia devices, mouse, keyboard, and smart card reader; monitor, configure, and troubleshoot multimedia hardware, such as cameras; install, configure, and manage modems; install, configure, and manage Infrared Data Association (IrDA) devices; install, configure, and manage wireless devices; install, configure, and manage USB devices, and install, configure, and manage hand held devices ... 64

3.4.2 Implement, manage, and troubleshoot input and output (I/O) devices; monitor, configure, and troubleshoot I/O devices, such as printers, scanners, multimedia devices, mouse, keyboard, and smart card reader; monitor, configure, and troubleshoot multimedia hardware, such as cameras; install, configure, and manage modems; install, configure, and manage wireless devices; install, configure, and manage USB devices; and install, configure, and manage hand held devices (cont) ... 66

3.5 Manage and troubleshoot drives and driver signing ... 68

3.6 Monitor and configure multiprocessor computers ... 70

SECTION 4 MONITORING AND OPTIMIZING SYSTEM PERFORMANCE AND RELIABILITY ... 73

4.1 Monitor, optimize, and troubleshoot performance of the Windows XP Professional desktop ... 74

4.1.1 Optimize and troubleshoot memory performance ... 76

4.1.2 Optimize and troubleshoot processor utilization ... 78

4.1.3 Optimize and troubleshoot disk performance ... 80

4.1.4 Optimize and troubleshoot application performance ... 82

4.1.5 Configure, manage, and troubleshoot Scheduled Tasks ... 84

4.2 Manage, monitor, and optimize system performance for mobile users ... 86

4.3 Restore and back up the operating system, system state data, and user data ... 88

4.3.1 Recover system state data and user data by using Windows Backup ... 90

4.3.2 Troubleshoot system restoration by starting in safe mode ... 92

4.3.3 Recover system state data and user data by using the Recovery Console ... 94

SECTION 5 CONFIGURING AND TROUBLESHOOTING THE DESKTOP ENVIRONMENT 97

    5.1 Configure and manage user profiles 98

    5.2 Configure support for multiple languages or multiple locations; enable multiple-language support; configure multiple-language support for users; configure local settings; configure Windows XP Professional for multiple locations 100

    5.3 Manage applications by using Windows Installer packages 102

    5.4 Configure and troubleshoot desktop settings 104

    5.5 Configure and troubleshoot accessibility services 106

SECTION 6 IMPLEMENTING, MANAGING, AND TROUBLESHOOTING NETWORK PROTOCOLS AND SERVICES 109

    6.1 Configure and troubleshoot the TCP/IP protocol 110

    6.2 Connect to computers by using dial-up networking; connect to computers by using a virtual private network (VPN) connection; create a dial-up connection to connect to a remote access server; connect to the Internet by using dial-up networking; and configure and troubleshoot Internet Connection Sharing 112

    6.3 Connect to resources using Internet Explorer 114

    6.4 Configure, manage, and implement Internet Information Services (IIS) 116

    6.5 Configure, manage, and troubleshoot remote desktop and remote assistance 118

    6.6 Configure, manage, and troubleshoot an Internet connection firewall 120

SECTION 7 CONFIGURING, MANAGING, AND TROUBLESHOOTING SECURITY 123

    7.1 Configure, manage, and troubleshoot Encrypting File System (EFS) 124

    7.2 Configure, manage, and troubleshoot local security policy 126

    7.3 Configure, manage, and troubleshoot local user and group accounts; configure and troubleshoot local users and groups; and configure, manage, and troubleshoot account settings 128

    7.3.1 Configure, manage, and troubleshoot auditing 130

    7.3.2 Configure, manage, and troubleshoot account policy 132

    7.3.3 Configure, manage, and troubleshoot user and group rights 134

    7.3.4 Troubleshoot cache credentials 136

    7.4 Configure, manage, and troubleshoot a security configuration 138

    7.5 Configure, manage, and troubleshoot Internet Explorer security settings 140

GLOSSARY OF ACRONYMS AND ABBREVIATIONS 143

ANSWER KEY 145

INDEX 161

PREFACE

The CoursePrep ExamGuide and CoursePrep StudyGuide are the very best tools to use to prepare for exam day. Both products provide thorough preparation for the MCSE 70-270: Installing, Configuring, and Administering Microsoft Windows XP Professional exam. These products are intended to be used with the core "Guide to" textbook, *MCSE Guide to Windows XP Professional*, (0-619-12031-2), by Ed Tittel and James Michael Stewart. CoursePrep ExamGuide and CoursePrep StudyGuide provide you ample opportunity to practice, drill, and rehearse for the exam!

COURSEPREP EXAMGUIDE

The *CoursePrep ExamGuide: MCSE Exam 70-270 for Windows XP Professional*, ISBN 0-619-12119-X, provides the essential information you need to master each exam objective. The ExamGuide devotes an entire two-page spread to each certification objective for this exam, helping you to understand the objective, and giving you the bottom line information—what you *really* need to know. Memorize these facts and bulleted points before heading into the exam. In addition, there are four to seven practice test questions for each objective on the right-hand page—over 250 questions total! CoursePrep ExamGuide provides the exam fundamentals and gets you up to speed quickly. If you are seeking even more opportunity to practice and prepare, we recommend that you consider our most complete solution, CoursePrep StudyGuide, which is described below.

COURSEPREP STUDYGUIDE

For those really serious about certification, we offer an even more robust solution—the *CoursePrep StudyGuide: MCSE Exam 70-270 for Windows XP Professional*, ISBN 0-619-12032-0. This offering includes all of the same great features you get with the CoursePrep ExamGuide, including the unique two-page spread, the bulleted memorization points, and the practice questions. In addition, you receive a password valid for six months of practice on CoursePrep, a dynamic test preparation tool. The password is found in an envelope in the back cover of the CoursePrep StudyGuide. CoursePrep is a Web-based pool of hundreds of sample test questions. CoursePrep exam simulation software mimics the exact exam environment. The CoursePrep software is flexible, and allows you to practice in several ways as you master the material. Choose from Certification Mode to experience actual exam-day conditions or Study Mode to request answers and explanations to practice questions. Custom Mode lets you set the options for the practice test, including number of questions, content coverage, and ability to request answers and explanations. Follow the instructions on the inside back cover to access the exam simulation software. To see a demo of this dynamic test preparation tool, go to *www.courseprep.com*.

FEATURES

The *CoursePrep ExamGuide* and *CoursePrep StudyGuide: MCSE Exam 70-270 for Microsoft Windows XP Professional* books include the following features:

Detailed coverage of the certification objectives in a unique two-page spread: Study strategically by really focusing in on the MCSE certification objectives. To enable you to do this, a two-page spread is devoted to each certification objective. The left-hand page provides the critical facts you need, while the right-hand page features practice questions relating to that objective. You'll find that the certification objective(s) and sub-objectives(s) are clearly listed in the upper left-hand corner of each spread.

An overview of the objective is provided in the ***Understanding the Objective*** section. Next, ***What you Really Need to Know*** lists bulleted, succinct facts, skills, and concepts about the objective. Memorizing these facts will be important for your success when taking the exam. ***Objectives on the Job*** places the objective in an industry perspective, and tells you how you can expect to utilize the objective on the job. This section also provides troubleshooting information.

Practice Test Questions: Each right-hand page contains four to seven practice test questions designed to help you prepare for the exam by testing your skills, identifying your strengths and weaknesses, and demonstrating the subject matter you will face on the exams and how it will be tested. These questions are written in a similar fashion to real MCSE exam questions. The questions test your knowledge of the objectives described on the left-hand page and also the information in the *MCSE Guide to Windows XP Professional* (ISBN 0-619-12031-2). You can find answers to the practice test questions in the answer key at the back of the book, and on the CoursePrep Web site, **www.courseprep.com**, where you can also find additional Web-based exam preparation questions.

Glossary: The glossary lists and defines acronyms that you need to know for the exams, and it is included in the back of the book as a reference.

How to Use This Book

The *CoursePrep ExamGuide* and *CoursePrep StudyGuide: MCSE Exam 70-270 for Microsoft Windows XP Professional* are all you need to successfully prepare for the MCSE certification exam if you have some experience and working knowledge of supporting and maintaining Microsoft Windows XP operating systems. This book is intended to be used with a core text, such as *MCSE Guide to Windows XP Professional (0-619-12031-2)*, also published by Course Technology. If you are new to this field, use this book as a roadmap for where you need to go to prepare for certification, and use the *MCSE Guide to Windows XP Professional* to give you the knowledge and understanding that you need to reach your goal. Course Technology publishes a full series of MCSE products that provide thorough preparation for all of the MCSE exams. For more information, visit our Web site at **www.course.com/networking**, or contact your sales representative.

For the most accurate and up-to-date information regarding the content of this book, see the Web-based errata at *www.lanw.com/books/errata*. E-mail comments about this book to *errata@lanw.com*, specifying the book title, ISBN, and page numbers.

Acknowledgments

We could not have completed this guide without the support and planning of the ever-capable and efficient Course Technology staff, especially Charles Blum, product manager, Steve Elliot, managing editor, and Danielle Power, production editor. Our sincere thanks to Christine Smith, the copy editor, for ensuring the clarity and consistency of the guide.

Acknowledgment from James Michael Stewart, Author:

Thanks to my boss, Ed Tittel, for the opportunity to write this book. Thanks to Kim Lindros and Dawn Rader, the best editors flattery can buy. To my parents, Dave and Sue, thanks for your love and consistent support. To my sister Sharon and my nephew Wesley, I've really enjoyed spending more time with you. To Mark, thanks for always having time to listen to me, providing encouragement, and understanding my sense of humor. To HERbert, it's back to just you and me kid—well, there is Quin, but now you've got someone else to play with. And finally, as always, to Elvis—your picture adorns my walls, my light switch covers, and my $2 bill—thanks for always giving a hunka-hunka burnin' HELLO!

Section 1

Installing Windows XP Professional

OBJECTIVES

1.1 Perform an attended installation of Windows XP Professional

WINDOWS XP PROFESSIONAL ATTENDED INSTALLATION

UNDERSTANDING THE OBJECTIVE

Windows XP Professional can be installed on a new system, as an upgrade over an existing operating system, as a replacement of an existing operating system (non-upgrade), or in a multiboot configuration with one or more existing operating systems. The attended installation process of Windows XP Professional is easy to follow, and it takes about one hour to complete.

WHAT YOU REALLY NEED TO KNOW

- System requirements: 233 MHz **CPU**, 128 MB **RAM**, 1.5 GB drive space, **SVGA** 800 x 600, CD-ROM/DVD drive, keyboard, and pointing device (optional). All other components should be **HCL**-compliant.
- To join a domain or workgroup during installation, an HCL-compliant **NIC** must be present in the computer.
- Windows XP can be an upgrade from Windows 98, Windows 98 SE, Windows Me, Windows NT Workstation 4.0 (with service packs), Windows 2000 Professional (with service packs), and Windows XP Home. Installing over any other operating system results in a full, clean installation.
- Windows XP installation can be started from a bootable local **CD-ROM/DVD** drive, or started manually from a local CD-ROM/DVD drive or from a network share of the distribution files.
- The setup utilities for Windows XP are located in the i386 directory on the distribution CD: WINNT and WINNT32. WINNT should be used on 16-bit operating systems; WINNT32 should be used on 32-bit operating systems.
- Dynamic update during installation can download new patches or components if Internet access is available.
- Windows XP must be activated within 30 days after installation. Activation prevents software piracy. Activation can occur over the Internet or by phone. After 30 days, the system prevents any access except to perform activation.
- Windows XP will install itself into the \WINDOWS folder on drive C: by default. To change this location, open the Advanced Options dialog box during the initial **GUI** section of setup (when started from an existing operating system) and mark the check box to select the destination partition during setup.

OBJECTIVES ON THE JOB

Installing Windows XP is a simple process; most users of previous Windows operating systems will be able to accomplish it easily. Attended installation does prompt several times for configuration details or option selections during installation. If you cannot stand by during installation or need to perform multiple installations, use an unattended installation method.

PRACTICE TEST QUESTIONS

1. Which of the following configuration elements would prevent the installation of Windows XP Professional?
   a. 300 MHz
   b. 64 MB RAM
   c. 2 GB drive space
   d. SVGA 800 x 600
   e. CD-RW/DVD drive

2. Which of the following operating systems are defined by Microsoft as valid upgradeable systems for Windows XP? (Choose all that apply.)
   a. Windows 98, SE, Windows Me
   b. Windows XP Home
   c. Windows 95
   d. Windows 2000 Professional (with service packs)
   e. Windows 2000 Server (with service packs)
   f. Windows NT Workstation 4.0 (with service packs)

3. To manually upgrade a Windows NT Workstation 4.0 system, what Windows XP Professional install utility should be used?
   a. WINNT
   b. WINNT32
   c. SETUP
   d. INSTALL

4. Dynamic update can download and integrate new patches or components during the initial installation of Windows XP if Internet access is available.
   a. True
   b. False

5. Windows XP must be activated within how many days after installation to allow access to the system?
   a. 12
   b. 15
   c. 30
   d. 60

6. What is the default destination of the Windows XP main system files?
   a. c:\WINNT
   b. c:\WINDOWS
   c. d:\winxp
   d. \\WINDOWS\xp

7. Windows XP can only be installed from a bootable local CD-ROM drive.
   a. True
   b. False

OBJECTIVES

1.2 Perform an unattended installation of Windows XP Professional

UNATTENDED INSTALLATION • UDF

UNDERSTANDING THE OBJECTIVE

Windows XP Professional offers many methods to perform an unattended installation. Unattended installations do not require a system operator to remain at the system while the install is being performed.

WHAT YOU REALLY NEED TO KNOW

- Windows XP offers several unattended installation methods, which include: using an answer file (see Object 1.2.3); using a uniqueness database file; using Remote Installation Services (see Objective 1.2.1); or using SYSPREP (see Objective 1.2.2).
- A **UDF** is used in conjunction with an unattended answer file. The uniqueness database file is a text file with the extension .udf. This file is used when multiple system installations using the same answer file require unique configuration information, such as **IP** address and system name.
- The UDF simplifies automating the installation on multiple systems. This simplification allows the same answer file to be used on each system instead of requiring a custom answer file to be created for each system.
- When a UDF and answer file are used, the data in the UDF takes precedence.
- To use a UDF, execute one of the following commands: WINNT /u:*answerfile.txt* /udf:*ID,filename.udf* or WINNT32 /unattend:<*answerfile.txt*>/udf:<*ID*>,<*filename*>.udf. The ID corresponds to an ID tag label within the UDF file. The ID tag label indicates which set of unique configuration settings should be employed on the current system.
- The following is a sample portion of a UDF:

```
[UniqueIDs]
     UserID1 = Userdata,GuiUnattended,Network
     UserID2 = Userdata,GuiUnattended,Network
  [UserID1:UserData]
  FullName = "Mark Gibson"
  ComputerName = "SalesFloor5"
  [UserID1:GuiUnattended]
  TimeZone = " (GMT-06:00) Central Time (US & Canada)"
```

OBJECTIVES ON THE JOB

When you cannot stand by a system during an installation or when you must perform numerous installs, use an unattended installation method. You must start an install, but no further action is required until the installation is completed. Automated installs require about an hour to complete.

PRACTICE TEST QUESTIONS

1. What mechanism is available to perform unattended installations of Windows XP Professional? (Choose all that apply.)
    a. Unattended answer files
    b. Remote Installation Services
    c. Manual network install
    d. SYSPREP

2. A UDF must be used with what unattended installation method?
    a. Answer file
    b. RIS
    c. SYSPREP
    d. SYSDIFF

3. A UDF is a:
    a. binary file containing unique configuration settings
    b. text file containing unique configuration settings
    c. binary file containing a complete set of configuration settings
    d. text file containing a complete set of configuration settings

4. The /udf syntax parameter can be used with: (Choose all that apply.)
    a. WINNT
    b. WINNT32
    c. SETUP
    d. INSTALL

5. What is used to point out a UDF's unique configuration settings that should be applied to a specific system?
    a. User name
    b. ID
    c. IP address
    d. Time stamp

6. A UDF enables the same answer file to be used on multiple system installations.
    a. True
    b. False

7. An automated installation is significantly quicker than a manual installation.
    a. True
    b. False

OBJECTIVES

1.2.1 Install Windows XP Professional by using Remote Installation Services (RIS)

INSTALLATION • RIS

UNDERSTANDING THE OBJECTIVE

Remote Installation Services is an excellent tool for deploying multiple clients on a medium-to-large domain. **RIS** offers a wide range of configuration settings and automation options.

WHAT YOU REALLY NEED TO KNOW

- Remote Installation Services is a Windows 2000 Server or Windows .NET Server service. Windows 2000 Server RIS is able to remotely install Windows 2000 Professional only. Windows .NET Server RIS is able to remotely install any version of Windows XP and Windows .NET remotely along with Windows 2000 Professional, Windows 2000 Server, and Windows 2000 Advanced Server. Windows 2000 Datacenter Server cannot be remotely installed with RIS.
- RIS is used to push operating system installations to remote systems.
- The destination system must meet all system requirements for the operating system to be installed. The destination system must also have either a RIS boot disk-supported NIC or **DHCP PXE**-based remote boot ROM NIC.
- RIS requires DHCP, **DNS**, and Active Directory within the domain.
- RIS installs can be fully automated or configured so end users can provide some or all of the necessary configuration settings.
- After an installation image is created on the RIS server, the destination system need only be loaded to initiate the installation process.

OBJECTIVES ON THE JOB

Remote Installation Services requires extensive planning and configuration to function effectively. RIS should be used when you must install a significant number of clients.

PRACTICE TEST QUESTIONS

1. Remote Installation Services can be used to remotely deploy any Microsoft operating system across a domain network.
    a. True
    b. False

2. RIS requires which of the following within a domain to support remote operating system deployments? (Choose all that apply.)
    a. DHCP
    b. WINS
    c. DNS
    d. Active Directory
    e. TCP/IP

3. Which of the following does the destination system require to receive an operating system installation via RIS?
    a. Windows .NET Server
    b. SCSI hard drive
    c. a RIS boot disk-supported NIC or a DHCP PXE-based remote boot ROM NIC

4. RIS installations can be fully automated, or they can require an end user to provide some or all configuration options during the setup process.
    a. True
    b. False

5. To initiate an RIS installation, what must be done at the destination client?
    a. Log on as Administrator.
    b. Start the Add or Remote Programs applet.
    c. Load the system.
    d. Disconnect from the network.

6. Windows XP Professional can be installed via RIS using either a Windows 2000 Server or a Windows .NET Server as the RIS host.
    a. True
    b. False

OBJECTIVES

1.2.2 Install Windows XP Professional by using the System Preparation Tool

INSTALLATION • SYSPREP

UNDERSTANDING THE OBJECTIVE

The System Preparation Tool, or **SYSPREP**, is a system preparation aid used when performing system duplication. System duplication, also known as cloning or imaging, requires a third-party tool such as Symantec's Ghost. SYSPREP prepares a system to be duplicated.

WHAT YOU REALLY NEED TO KNOW

- ◆ System duplication can create multiple exact duplicates of a system, including the installed operating system, applications, and all configuration settings.
- ◆ SYSPREP is used as follows: First, a master system is configured with an operating system, applications, and any custom settings. Second, SYSPREP is executed on that system and then powers down that system. Third, a drive imaging or cloning tool is used to create copies of the prepared system drive. Finally, the original system or any clones are booted.
- ◆ When the original system or clones are booted for the first time, the operating system rescans the system using Plug and Play and attempts to reconfigure all discovered hardware. The operating system might prompt for information or drivers if they cannot be located automatically.
- ◆ The destination systems for a cloned image must consist of compatible components which are similar to the original system. Using core components that require different device drivers than those present on the original system will result in a clone failure.
- ◆ System duplication cannot be used to perform an upgrade installation. Instead, system duplication can be used to install a clone of the original system on an empty volume, or to overwrite an existing volume hosting an operating system.
- ◆ A Sysprep.inf file can be used with cloned images to provide configuration details that either are not determined upon bootup and system inspection or that are specifically different from the original system. A Sysprep.inf file can be created by Setup Manager in the same manner as the Unattend.txt file.

OBJECTIVES ON THE JOB

SYSPREP and drive-cloning tools are excellent means by which to duplicate configured systems. Copying a drive takes about as long as performing an operating system install. However, because the clone will include applications and custom configurations, this method saves time overall.

PRACTICE TEST QUESTIONS

1. **SYSPREP is used to clone systems.**
   a. True
   b. False

2. **SYSPREP must be used with what other tool?**
   a. Setup Manager
   b. WINNT32
   c. Drive-cloning utility
   d. Remote Installation Services

3. **The SYSPREP installation mechanism is used to duplicate what component on a system? (Choose all that apply.)**
   a. Operating system
   b. Applications
   c. Physical RAM
   d. Custom configuration

4. **What file can be used to provide additional configuration information on clones when SYSPREP is used?**
   a. Unattend.txt
   b. Sysprep.udf
   c. Setup.log
   d. Sysprep.inf

5. **The SYSPREP mechanism can be used to perform: (Choose all that apply.)**
   a. upgrade installations
   b. installations on a new system with clean drives
   c. installations over an existing operating system on a system

6. **Which system will rescan for hardware upon bootup when SYSPREP is used? (Choose all that apply.)**
   a. All client systems
   b. Original system
   c. Cloned systems
   d. Only non-domain controllers

7. **The destination systems for a cloned image must consist of compatible components that are similar to the original system.**
   a. True
   b. False

OBJECTIVES

1.2.3 Create unattended answer files by using Setup Manager to automate the installation of Windows XP Professional

SETUP MANAGER

UNDERSTANDING THE OBJECTIVE

Setup Manager is a wizard tool used to quickly create answer files for various types of installation mechanisms.

WHAT YOU REALLY NEED TO KNOW

- Setup Manager can be used to create answer files for an unattended installation, a system prep installation, or a RIS installation.
- Setup Manager must be manually installed on your system from the \Support\Tools\Deploy.cab file located on the Windows XP Professional distribution CD.
- Setup Manager can edit an existing answer file or it can be used to create a new answer file.
- Setup Manager from the Windows XP Professional CD can create answer files for Windows XP Home, Windows XP Professional, Windows .NET Server, Advanced Server, or Datacenter Server. However, the Setup Manager interface labels .NET as "2002."
- Setup Manager can create several types of answer files such as: provide defaults for a manually traversed install (this type allows the user to change supplied data); a fully automated install; hide specific pages of the install process and provide data for those hidden pages; read-only defaults for a manually traversed install; and a GUI-attended install where the text-mode portions of install are predefined.
- Setup Manager can create an answer file and customize a distribution folder, or create an answer file for installation from a CD. Customizing a distribution folder can include the incorporation of device drivers.
- The answer file can also contain instructions to preinstall printers (local and network); execute a command, batch file, or program after installation is completed; or execute a command, batch file, or program the first time a user logs on.

OBJECTIVES ON THE JOB

Setup Manager greatly simplifies the process of creating answer files, and it completely prevents syntax errors.

PRACTICE TEST QUESTIONS

1. **Setup Manager can be used to create answer files for: (Choose all that apply.)**
    a. RIS
    b. SYSPREP
    c. the Files and Settings Transfer Wizard
    d. unattended installs

2. **Setup Manager is installed by default as a Control Panel applet.**
    a. True
    b. False

3. **Setup Manager can be used to: (Choose all that apply.)**
    a. create new answer files
    b. create answer files by examining an existing system
    c. edit existing answer files
    d. force an existing system to comply with an answer file

4. **Setup Manager from the Windows XP Professional CD can create answer files to install which operating system? (Choose all that apply.)**
    a. Windows XP
    b. Windows NT
    c. Windows 2000
    d. Windows .NET

5. **Setup Manager can create several types of answer files, such as: (Choose all that apply.)**
    a. defaults only
    b. high security
    c. fully automated
    d. voice command
    e. read only
    f. hide pages
    g. GUI only

6. **Setup Manager can create a customized distribution folder along with an answer file to address special configurations, such as new devices with newly released device drivers.**
    a. True
    b. False

7. **An answer file can be used to perform several actions that a normal or manual installation process does not offer, such as: (Choose all that apply.)**
    a. preinstall printers
    b. join a domain
    c. execute commands on first logon
    d. install NWLink
    e. execute batch files after installation is completed

OBJECTIVES

1.3 Upgrade from a previous version of Windows to Windows XP Professional

UPGRADING TO WINDOWS XP PROFESSIONAL

UNDERSTANDING THE OBJECTIVE

Windows XP Professional can be installed as an upgrade from certain previous versions of Windows. Performing an upgrade will retain much of the current configuration and user data.

WHAT YOU REALLY NEED TO KNOW

- ◆ Windows XP Professional can be installed as an upgrade over Windows 98, Windows 98 SE, Windows Me, Windows XP Home, Windows NT Workstation 4.0 (with service packs), and Windows 2000 Professional (with service packs).
- ◆ For an upgrade to succeed, the computer must meet the minimum requirements for Windows XP Professional.
- ◆ An upgrade installation over Windows 95 can be attempted, but Microsoft does not officially list this operating system as an upgrade path. Windows 95 is no longer supported by Microsoft, so any success or failure with upgrading Windows 95 is the responsibility of the consumer. You may perform a clean installation over Windows 95.
- ◆ Windows XP Professional cannot be installed as an upgrade over Windows 3.x, Windows NT Server 4.0, Windows 2000 Server, or any outdated Windows versions. Instead of an upgrade, a full, clean installation can be performed over these operating systems to replace the current operating system, or the installation can occur on a second partition/volume to create a multi-boot computer.
- ◆ Upgrading from a previous operating system to Windows XP Professional will retain as much user configuration and preference settings as possible. Typically this means the network configuration, installed applications, and desktop environment customizations (such as color scheme, sounds, wallpaper, and screen saver) will be retained.
- ◆ You can perform an upgrade installation of Windows XP Professional over an existing installation of Windows XP Professional. Performing an upgrade can be useful for troubleshooting. If the system is not functioning properly, an upgrade may replace damaged or misconfigured components and restore the system to proper working order.
- ◆ An upgrade installation is initiated by selecting Upgrade from the drop-down list on the first screen of the Setup Wizard when WINNT or WINNT32 is started. The upgrade process is usually quicker than a full installation; it attempts to extract necessary configuration data from the existing system. Any data item that cannot be discovered will require your input.

OBJECTIVES ON THE JOB

Performing an upgrade to Windows XP Professional from a previous version of Windows is usually an intelligent choice in a networked office environment. Retaining as much of the users' previous environments speeds their familiarity and use of the new operating system.

PRACTICE TEST QUESTIONS

1. Which of the following systems can be upgraded to Windows XP Professional?
    a. Windows XP Home on a 180 MHz 128 MB RAM system
    b. Windows Me on a 300 MHz 128 MB RAM system
    c. Windows 2000 Professional on a 233 MHz 64 MB RAM system
    d. Windows NT Server 4.0 on a 300 MHz 256 MB RAM system

2. If a previous version of Windows, supported as an upgrade path for Windows XP Professional, is installed on a computer that does not meet Windows XP Professional minimum system requirements, the upgrade can still be performed successfully.
    a. True
    b. False

3. Which of the following operating systems cannot be upgraded to Windows XP Professional? (Choose all that apply.)
    a. Windows 98 SE
    b. Windows 2000 Server
    c. Windows 3.1
    d. Windows NT Workstation 4.0

4. The upgrade process always resets the network configuration of a system.
    a. True
    b. False

5. Performing an upgrade installation over an existing Windows XP Professional system that is not functioning properly may result in repairing the system.
    a. True
    b. False

6. Windows XP Professional can only be installed as an upgrade when using the Winnt.exe command to initiate the installation.
    a. True
    b. False

7. An upgrade installation that is successful still requires the reinstallation of all applications.
    a. True
    b. False

OBJECTIVES

1.3.1 Prepare a computer to meet upgrade requirements

UPGRADE REQUIREMENTS

UNDERSTANDING THE OBJECTIVE

Windows XP Professional has specific system requirements. If these requirements are not satisfied at the time of installation, the setup process will terminate. You must ensure that your system is fully capable of supporting Windows XP Professional before attempting an installation.

WHAT YOU REALLY NEED TO KNOW

- Windows XP Professional requires that the host computer meet specific system requirements. These are: 233 MHz CPU, 128 MB RAM, 1.5 GB drive space, SVGA 800 x 600, CD-ROM/DVD drive, keyboard, and a pointing device (optional).
- All components should be HCL-compliant. Non-HCL-compliant devices might not function under Windows XP or might cause Windows XP to function improperly or erratically.
- The HCL is actively maintained by Microsoft online to reflect the latest devices and device drivers available. To access the HCL, go to *http://www.microsoft.com/hcl*.
- If you have hardware that requires drivers not present on the Windows XP Professional distribution CD, be sure to have them available on CD or floppy.
- If you need dial-up Internet access, install an HCL-compliant 14.4 Kbps or higher speed modem.
- If you need LAN network access, install an HCL-compliant NIC.
- If you need voice and video conferencing, install an HCL-compliant 33.6 Kbps or higher speed modem or a network connection, a sound card, a microphone, speakers or a headset, and a digital video camera.
- If you need application sharing, install an HCL-compliant 33.6 Kbps or higher speed modem or a network connection.
- If you need audio capabilities, install an HCL-compliant sound card and speakers or a headset.
- If you need DVD playback capabilities, install an HCL-compliant DVD player, 8 MB or more video RAM, and have DVD decoder software available.
- If you need to use Windows Movie Maker, you will need an HCL-compliant digital or analog video capture device.

OBJECTIVES ON THE JOB

You must meet the minimum system requirements for Windows XP Professional to install and use the operating system. Install as much capability in a system as possible—purchase the most powerful system you can afford and be sure to fully populate the RAM.

PRACTICE TEST QUESTIONS

1. What are the minimum system requirements for Windows XP Professional?
    a. 233 MHz CPU, 128 MB RAM, 1.5 GB drive space
    b. 300 MHz CPU, 64 MB RAM, 500 MB drive space
    c. 450 MHz CPU, 256 MB RAM, 1 GB drive space

2. Windows XP Professional will not install if a single component is not HCL-compatible.
    a. True
    b. False

3. If a computer fails to meet the minimum system requirements for Windows XP, the installation process will complete but the operating system will perform erratically.
    a. True
    b. False

4. For LAN network access, a Windows XP Professional system must meet minimum system requirements and requires a:
    a. 14.4 Kbps modem
    b. NIC
    c. sound card
    d. DVD drive

5. For dial-up Internet access, a Windows XP Professional system must meet minimum system requirements and also requires a minimum of a:
    a. 14.4 Kbps modem
    b. NIC
    c. sound card
    d. 33.6 Kbps modem

6. For application sharing, a Windows XP Professional system must meet minimum system requirements and also requires a: (Choose all that apply.)
    a. 33.6 Kbps modem
    b. NIC
    c. sound card
    d. digital video camera

7. For Windows Movie Maker, a Windows XP Professional system must meet minimum system requirements and also requires a:
    a. digital or analog video capture device
    b. NIC
    c. sound card
    d. DVD drive

OBJECTIVES

1.3.2 Migrate existing user environments to a new installation

USER ENVIRONMENT MIGRATION

UNDERSTANDING THE OBJECTIVE

Migrating the user environment to Windows XP Professional involves one or more of several features or tools. These include roaming user profiles, the upgrade installation process, and the File and Settings Transfer Wizard.

WHAT YOU REALLY NEED TO KNOW

- Roaming user profiles are designed to create a consistent user environment on any client computer a particular user selects to log on to. A roaming user profile contains a wide range of user-specific data, including e-mail configuration, color scheme, favorites, and histories.
- Windows XP roaming user profiles are compatible with Windows 2000 systems, but not compatible with Windows 9x or NT systems. When moving from a Windows XP system to a Windows 9x or NT system, the user will be given a default blank user profile instead of their Windows XP roaming user profile.
- Upgrading from a previous operating system to Windows XP Professional will migrate system and user environment settings. The migration of data will only occur from valid upgrade paths.
- The Files and Settings Transfer Wizard can be used to migrate user environmental settings and personal data from Windows 95 (although the upgrade is not supported), Windows 98, Windows 98 SE, Windows Me, Windows NT, Windows 2000, or Windows XP systems to a new Windows XP Professional system.
- The Files and Settings Transfer Wizard is within the System Tools subfolder of the Start menu on Windows XP systems, and it is on the distribution CD in the \Support\Tools folder as Fastwiz.exe. If the CD is not available, you can create a wizard disk through the Files and Settings Transfer Wizard itself.
- The Files and Settings Transfer Wizard must be executed on the old system to select the components and data files to move to the new system. The wizard will create a large dataset that can be stored on a network share or burned onto a CD (if less than 650 MB). The dataset can be quite large. The default settings grab nearly every non-native Windows file on the system.
- Once the dataset is created, the wizard is executed on the new system to import the settings and place the data files in folders.

OBJECTIVES ON THE JOB

The File and Settings Transfer Wizard is an excellent means by which to migrate older client system environments to Windows XP Professional systems. You can use the wizard to retain user configurations from pre-Windows 98 operating systems in spite of the upgrade restrictions.

PRACTICE TEST QUESTIONS

1. What mechanism can be used to transfer user environmental settings from one system to another? (Choose all that apply.)
    a. Files and Settings Transfer Wizard
    b. Remote Installation Services
    c. Roaming user profiles
    d. Upgrade installations

2. Windows XP roaming user profiles can be used on what type of system?
    a. Windows 95
    b. Windows NT
    c. Windows 2000
    d. Windows 98

3. Performing an upgrade installation will retain user environmental settings when installing Windows XP Professional on a system that previously hosted Windows 3.1.
    a. True
    b. False

4. The Files and Settings Transfer Wizard must always be executed from the Windows XP Professional distribution CD.
    a. True
    b. False

5. A wizard disk contains the dataset to be moved from the old system to the new system.
    a. True
    b. False

6. A wizard disk is created by executing the makeboot file from the Windows XP Professional distribution CD.
    a. True
    b. False

7. The defaults of the Files and Settings Transfer Wizard, when creating the dataset to move from the old system to the new system, attempt to grab nearly every non-native Windows file on the computer.
    a. True
    b. False

OBJECTIVES

1.4 Perform post-installation updates and product activation

POST-INSTALLATION UPDATES • PRODUCT ACTIVATION

UNDERSTANDING THE OBJECTIVE

Microsoft periodically releases updates to their products that correct programming bugs, improve operation, or fix security holes. Windows XP Professional includes an update mechanism to automate this function and keep your system up to date. Windows XP must be activated.

WHAT YOU REALLY NEED TO KNOW

- Windows XP Professional must be activated within 30 days after the initial installation. Activation is a new antipiracy tool that requires you to contact Microsoft to associate your computer with a legally purchased copy of Windows XP.
- Activation is different than registration. Registering with Microsoft is optional; activation is mandatory.
- After the activation time limit expires, the operating system will not function other than to allow you to perform an activation.
- Activation can occur over the Internet or over the phone.
- Activation can take place during initial installation or by starting the Activate Windows tool from the Start menu.
- Windows Update is a tool that downloads and installs patches to the operating system. Windows Update connects to the Microsoft Web site to determine whether your system has all the recommended or available patches installed.
- Windows Update can be started from the Start menu or from the Tools menu of Internet Explorer.
- The Automatic Updates tab of the System applet is used to configure the automation of Windows Update. You can configure Windows XP to download all updates automatically and notify the user when they are ready to be installed, notify before downloading and again when ready to install, or turn off automatic update completely.
- If you decline to install an update and then later decide you want to install it, you can click the Restore Declined Updates button on the Automatic Updates tab of the System applet to access a list of refused updates and re-enable them.

OBJECTIVES ON THE JOB

Product activation will help reduce piracy of Windows XP; however, it can pose problems when you make significant changes to a computer. If you replace more than six components, Windows XP may think you've copied XP onto a new system and will force you to reactivate. Keeping current with updates through Windows Update and Automatic Updates is a good idea, especially if you are connected to the Internet or working from a network.

PRACTICE TEST QUESTIONS

1. Windows XP Professional must be activated with _____ days.
    a. five
    b. 15
    c. 30
    d. 45

2. Product activation is a means to prevent:
    a. increased sales
    b. upgrading
    c. piracy
    d. Internet conferencing

3. Product activation can occur through what means? (Choose all that apply.)
    a. Online
    b. With any PC manufacturer
    c. Using floppies
    d. Over the telephone

4. After the time limit for product activation expires and you have failed to activate Windows XP, what occurs?
    a. You are forced to reinstall the operating system.
    b. You are allowed access to the local system but not to networked resources.
    c. You are allowed only to perform activation.
    d. You must purchase a new user license.

5. Windows Update is used to perform an upgrade from a previous operating system.
    a. True
    b. False

6. Automatic Updates can be configured to automatically download and install all updates released by Microsoft.
    a. True
    b. False

7. After an update has been refused, it cannot be reactivated.
    a. True
    b. False

OBJECTIVES

1.5 Troubleshoot failed installations

INSTALLATION TROUBLESHOOTING

UNDERSTANDING THE OBJECTIVE

The Windows XP Professional installation process is fairly reliable. However, in those cases when an installation error occurs, there are several steps you can take to remedy the situation.

WHAT YOU REALLY NEED TO KNOW

- One cause of installation termination is to attempt an install on a system that does not meet minimum system requirements. To correct this, install the necessary hardware and start over.
- If an installation fails or hangs, restart the system to allow the setup process to start over. If it fails again, double-check that all of your hardware is HCL-compliant and that it is all fully operational.
- If the installation process claims a specific file cannot be copied or is corrupted, double-check that your distribution source is intact. If your CD has a scratch on it, if you failed to copy every file to a network distribution point, or if your network distribution point has been altered (that is, it has deleted files, infected files, corrupted files, or bad sectors), you should obtain the distribution files again. This type of error is known as a media error.
- If you are unable to join the domain during installation, check physical cable connections and verify the following: the domain controller is online; you have provided the client with correct network configuration parameters; other clients can access the domain controller; and you are using an HCL-compliant NIC.
- If a stop error occurs (recognizable by the blue screen dump message), either a hardware problem or a bad driver is involved. Hardware problems can be resolved by replacing non-HCL-compliant devices or replacing failing devices. Bad drivers should be replaced with current updated drivers from the device vendor.
- Dependency failures typically occur after installation is completed. A dependency failure is actually multiple failures that occur because of a single issue. If a key service fails to execute upon bootup, all services, drivers, and applications that require that service will fail as well. For example, if the NIC driver fails to load, then the Server and Workstation services will fail, and in turn it will not be possible to share resources with or access resources over the network. Dependency failures can be detected by viewing the System Log in Event Viewer. Error or warning event details should be examined and steps taken to prevent their future recurrence.

OBJECTIVES ON THE JOB

Installation problems with Windows XP Professional are rare. But when they do occur, the cause almost always related to bad hardware or a bad device driver. Using only HCL-compliant devices and having the correct device drivers available (if not already present on the Windows XP Professional distribution CD) will prevent most installation failures.

PRACTICE TEST QUESTIONS

1. **What is the most common cause of installation failures?**
    a. Missing NIC
    b. Non-HCL-compliant hardware
    c. Insufficient drive space
    d. Not enough RAM

2. **The setup process will self-terminate if it detects which of the following conditions?**
    a. Presence of an HCL-compliant sound card
    b. No network connectivity
    c. Insufficient RAM
    d. Over 16 GB of drive space in a single partition

3. **What is the best first course of action to take if the setup process hangs?**
    a. Locate new distribution media.
    b. Check the Event Viewer.
    c. Replace core hardware devices.
    d. Restart the system.

4. **Windows XP Professional cannot be installed if the setup process cannot communicate with a domain controller.**
    a. True
    b. False

5. **A stop error during installation is usually caused by:**
    a. the presence of SCSI hard drives
    b. dependency errors
    c. use of non-HCL-compliant devices
    d. not activating Windows XP

6. **A dependency failure is a failure that occurs upon bootup, and in turn causes all services, drivers, and applications that require that service to fail as well.**
    a. True
    b. False

7. **All media errors can be corrected by restarting the destination system and reinitiating the installation process.**
    a. True
    b. False

Section 2

Implementing and Conducting Administration of Resources

OBJECTIVES

2.1 Monitor, manage, and troubleshoot access to files and folders

ACCESS MONITORING • ACCESS MANAGEMENT • ACCESS TROUBLESHOOTING

UNDERSTANDING THE OBJECTIVE

Monitoring access is the ability to know what resources are being accessed by which users at any given moment. Managing access is the ability to share resources and terminate access as needed. Troubleshooting access is the ability to resolve problems encountered by users attempting to interact with a resource.

WHAT YOU REALLY NEED TO KNOW

- It is possible to monitor current shared folder resource access statistics through the Shared Folders section of Computer Management (a tool found in Administrative Tools). This tool displays all shares from the local system (including administrative shares), all sessions with remote users accessing shared folders, and a list of all files being used during active sessions.
- From the Sessions subnode of Shared Folders, current sessions can be terminated by issuing the Close Session command from the Action menu. Terminating a session closes open files associated with that session.
- From the Open Files subnode of Shared Folders, open files can be closed by issuing the Close Open File command from the Action menu.
- Access management takes the form of properly assigning access permissions to users and groups for the shared resource and limiting the number of simultaneous users of that resource.
- Access to resources is managed by electing whether to share a resource with the network and defining the access restrictions for the shared resource. See Objective 2.1.2 for controlling resource access with permissions.
- Problems with access are typically related to a problem with network connectivity or to incorrectly defined access permissions. See Objective 2.1.2 for troubleshooting access permissions. Once connectivity is examined and verified, attempt to access the resource with an administrator account or from different systems. If problems persist, delete and re-create the share.
- Keep in mind that shares can be set to allow a maximum number of simultaneous users. When the maximum user level is reached, all additional attempts will be denied. The connection failed error caused by this can be mistaken for a real problem instead of just a connection throttle limitation.

OBJECTIVES ON THE JOB

There are few tools available native to Windows XP Professional which can be used to monitor, manage, and troubleshoot access. In most cases, these actions use seat-of-the-pants methods or just common sense. Don't forget that access problems can also occur when the resource owner disables sharing or the host system is offline.

PRACTICE TEST QUESTIONS

1. **Through the Shared Folders section of Computer Management, it is possible to: (Choose all that apply.)**
    a. disconnect active sessions
    b. send messages to users
    c. close open files
    d. define access permissions

2. **The Shared Folders section of Computer Management displays: (Choose all that apply.)**
    a. all shares on the network
    b. all local shares
    c. all nonadministrative shares
    d. only administrative shares

3. **Terminating an active session will also close all open files associated with that session.**
    a. True
    b. False

4. **Controlling access to resources can involve which of the following activities? (Choose all that apply.)**
    a. sharing a resource
    b. altering user group memberships
    c. defining access permissions
    d. setting maximum simultaneous user limits
    e. transforming a basic storage drive into a dynamic storage drive

5. **Problems with connectivity can often be tied to which of the following? (Choose all that apply.)**
    a. Client operating system
    b. Network connectivity
    c. Fast user switching
    d. Access permission settings

6. **When the maximum number of simultaneous users is reached on a share, the next user attempting access to that same share will see a message stating the maximum number of users for this share has been reached and to try again later.**
    a. True
    b. False

7. **Actively monitoring the Open Files subnode of Shared Folders is a better control mechanism than restriction access based on group membership to shares.**
    a. True
    b. False

OBJECTIVES

2.1.1 Configure, manage, and troubleshoot file compression

FILE COMPRESSION

UNDERSTANDING THE OBJECTIVE

File compression is supported by **NTFS** under Windows XP the same as it is under Windows 2000. File compression is on a file, folder, or drive basis. Windows XP also includes a native zipping tool that creates .zip files (also known as compressed folders).

WHAT YOU REALLY NEED TO KNOW

- File compression is enabled on a file or folder basis through the Advanced button on a file system object's Properties dialog box. Marking the Compress contents to save disk space check box enables compression.
- Entire drives can be compressed by marking the Compress drive to save disk space check box on the General tab of a volume/partition's Properties dialog box.
- When compression is enabled on a folder, you are prompted whether to compress just the selected folder or the folder, its contents, and all subfolders and their contents.
- Once compression is enabled for specific files and folders, there are no further configuration settings or user controls. The operating system manages all compression and decompression automatically.
- Files and folders are compressed only while they reside on the hard drive. After they are read into memory for use by an application, the operating system decompresses them as they are read from the drive.
- Compression is a file system object attribute. The inheritance rules of a moved file versus a copied file are the same as any other file system object attribute.
- To troubleshoot compression, first attempt to reverse the compression status of the suspect file object. Second, restart the system—this might reset memory errors that prevented proper reading of a compressed file.
- File system objects that are compressed cannot be encrypted. Compression and encryption are mutually exclusive.
- Compressing folders is an alternative to file compression, which creates a .zip file that contains compressed contents. Compressed folders can be stored on either **FAT** or NTFS volumes or transferred to other systems. Compressed folders can be copied, deleted, added to, or extracted from, just like a normal folder. A compressed folder can be protected with a password. Compressed folders can be opened on other non-XP systems using any standard .zip file extraction tool.

OBJECTIVES ON THE JOB

Compressed file system objects can be displayed in a different color (typically blue) than normal objects or encrypted objects. This setting is made on the View tab of the Folder Options applet. Working with highly compressed drives or collections of file system objects may result in noticeable system slowdown due to the time required to decompress objects as they are accessed.

PRACTICE TEST QUESTIONS

1. Windows XP Professional offers file compression in what denomination? (Choose all that apply.)
   a. File by file
   b. Folders and their contents
   c. All files of a specified type
   d. Entire drives

2. A single file can be compressed and encrypted at the same time.
   a. True
   b. False

3. Using compression extensively can negatively affect system performance.
   a. True
   b. False

4. When compressing a folder, which of the following occurs?
   a. The folder and its contents are compressed by default.
   b. Only the folder is compressed by default.
   c. You are prompted whether to compress only the folder or the folder and its contents.
   d. An error occurs because folders cannot be compressed.

5. Which of the following is true of compressed folders? (Choose all that apply.)
   a. They can be stored on FAT volumes
   b. They can be stored on NTFS volumes
   c. They cannot be stored on floppies
   d. They can be attached to e-mails
   e. They can be distributed to other systems
   f. They require Windows XP to extract and view contents
   g. They can be protected by passwords
   h. They act in the same manner as folders when moved, copied, added to, or extracted from

6. Troubleshooting compression problems can take the form of: (Choose all that apply.)
   a. reversing the state of compression on the problematic files and folders
   b. reinstalling Windows XP
   c. restarting the system
   d. deleting the problematic file

7. If a compressed file is moved from c:\documents to c:\storage, and the former folder is compressed but the latter is not, what happens to the moved file? (Choose all that apply.)
   a. It will remain compressed.
   b. It will be decompressed.
   c. It will inherit the settings of its new parent folder.
   d. It will retain the settings of its previous location.

OBJECTIVES

2.1.2 Control access to files and folders by using permissions

CONTROLLING ACCESS WITH PERMISSIONS

UNDERSTANDING THE OBJECTIVE

Security under Windows XP is primarily managed through the use of permissions.

WHAT YOU REALLY NEED TO KNOW

- Permissions are assigned to file system objects. Permissions define which users and groups have access to an object. Permissions define the type of actions or services that users and groups can perform on or with the object.
- File objects have six default permissions: Full Control, Modify, Read & Execute, Read, Write, and Special Permissions.
- Folder objects have seven default permissions: Full Control, Modify, Read & Execute, List Folder Contents, Read, Write, and Special Permissions.
- Permissions are defined for users and groups on an Allow or Deny basis.
- A user must have a specifically defined permission for an object; he or she is not granted access by default. If a user has a specifically defined Deny permission for an attempted type of action or service, that action or service is denied. If the user has a specifically defined Allow permission for an attempted type of action or service, that action or service is granted.
- The permission settings on file system objects control both local and remote (through share) access. For details on share permissions and their effect on remote access, see Objective 2.2.1.
- A Deny setting always overrides or trumps any other setting, even across group memberships for the same object.
- A user's access permissions are the cumulative total of all of that user's group and specific user permissions.
- Newly created volumes always default to Full Control to the Everyone group.
- There are 14 advanced permissions that can be used to customize access permissions on a finer scale than the default permissions offered on file system objects.
- Inheritance is the process by which a child object inherits settings from a parent object. By default, child objects inherit settings from parent containers. Advanced settings allow inheritance to be disabled, can force child propagation (that is, override non-inheritance settings on child objects), or can custom-define inheritance patterns (such as folder and subfolders, folder and files, subfolders only, and files only).

OBJECTIVES ON THE JOB

Access permissions are managed through planning, intelligently mapping out groups, and then assigning users to groups and assigning access permissions to objects using those groups.

PRACTICE TEST QUESTIONS

1. **Access permission is assigned only on a per-user basis.**
    a. True
    b. False

2. **The Microsoft recommended scheme for controlling access is to place users in groups, and then assign groups access permissions to objects.**
    a. True
    b. False

3. **What setting always supercedes all other settings?**
    a. Allow
    b. Deny
    c. Disable inheritance
    d. Set inheritance to files only

4. **The actual access permissions a user has for a particular object is determined by:**
    a. looking only at access permissions specifically defined for his user account
    b. default. All users always have full control access to all local resources
    c. cumulating all access permissions granted the user account through group memberships and specifically assigned to the user account
    d. cumulating all Deny permissions set against the user account or any group memberships, then taking the inverse

5. **Newly created volumes have what access permissions set by default?**
    a. Full Control to the Administrators group
    b. Read access to the Users group
    c. Read & Execute and Write access to the Users group
    d. Full Control to the Everyone group

6. **Child objects always inherit the settings of their parent container by default.**
    a. True
    b. False

7. **There are 14 advanced permissions that can be used to customize access permissions on a finer scale than the default permissions offered on file system objects.**
    a. True
    b. False

OBJECTIVES

2.1.3 Optimize access to files and folders

ACCESS OPTIMIZATION

UNDERSTANDING THE OBJECTIVE

Optimizing access to files and folders takes planning and careful implementation.

WHAT YOU REALLY NEED TO KNOW

- Access optimization is usually focused on improving the access experience of a user when connecting to resources over a network. To improve this experience, both the network-related components and file-related components must be addressed.
- Order the bindings for the network connection over which resources are accessed so that the preferred or most commonly used protocols and services are priorities.
- The host of the resources to be accessed should perform as few operations as possible. A server or client with the single task of sharing resources will offer faster service than one that is performing several other tasks simultaneously.
- To improve access, groups and individual users should carefully be assigned proper access permissions. Access permissions must be defined both on shares and on NTFS file system-level objects. Grant access necessary to perform required job tasks only to those users or groups who need access.
- You can limit the number of simultaneous users to a shared resource by changing the User limit from Maximum allowed to Allow this number of users, and by defining a specific number. This change is made on the Sharing tab of a shared resource.
- Resource access can also be optimized through enabling remote systems to cache a copy of a shared resource. A cached resource is accessed more quickly because it does not require communication over the network to request the resource or to transfer the resource to the requesting client. The benefit of caching occurs only after a resource has first been requested from its original source, and then cached locally.
- Caching of resources can be configured to allow manual caching of documents (enabled by default), automatic caching of documents, or automatic caching of programs and documents. You configure this setting by clicking the Caching button on the Sharing tab of a shared resource. Manual caching is performed through the Offline Files utility on a client system.
- Use the automatic caching of programs and documents setting only with read-only data and network-executed applications.

OBJECTIVES ON THE JOB

Optimizing access is primarily an issue when resource-hosting systems are slow to respond to access requests or when the network is heavily loaded. In most cases, shared resource access is almost as fast as accessing local resources. However, when an access delay is noticeable, the actions required to improve performance may be justified.

PRACTICE TEST QUESTIONS

1. Access optimization is achieved by reducing or eliminating the time lag between the moment a user requests a resource and when a remote system provides that resource.
   a. True
   b. False

2. Access optimization can involve improving or fine-tuning which component? (Choose all that apply.)
   a. Access permissions
   b. Network connectivity
   c. Simultaneous users
   d. Host system resource utilization
   e. Roaming user profile

3. Network connectivity can often be improved by adjusting the binding order.
   a. True
   b. False

4. When pulling resources from systems with poor network connectivity, such as those accessed over a VPN Internet link, what steps should be taken to optimize access for individual users? (Choose all that apply.)
   a. Grant Full Control to the Everyone group.
   b. Restrict maximum number of simultaneous users.
   c. Disable all shares.
   d. Use IPSec.
   e. Enable resource caching.

5. When does caching offer improved or optimized resource access? (Choose all that apply.)
   a. When the resource changes
   b. During the first access of a resource
   c. During an access repetition of the resource
   d. When the client system (that is, the system from which a user is requesting access to a shared resource) is offline

6. The automatic caching of programs and documents setting should only be used with read-only data and network-executed applications.
   a. True
   b. False

7. Using permissions to restrict access to popular resources to only users and groups who actually need the resource can optimize access for authorized users.
   a. True
   b. False

OBJECTIVES

2.2 Manage and troubleshoot access to shared folders; create and remove shared folders; control access to shared folders by using permissions

SHARED FOLDERS

UNDERSTANDING THE OBJECTIVE

Shared folders is the primary means by which file resources on one system are made available to other systems on a network. Managing shares is not a difficult task, but it does require planning.

WHAT YOU REALLY NEED TO KNOW

- ◆ Shared folder management has three primary components: creating the share, defining permissions, and limiting simultaneous access.
- ◆ On domain member Windows XP clients, you create a shared folder by marking the Share this folder radio button and providing a share name on the Sharing tab of the folder's Properties dialog box. By default, a new share's permissions are set to Full Control to the Everyone group and have an unrestricted limitation on simultaneous users. To terminate a share, return to the Sharing tab of the folder's Properties dialog box and select the Do not share this folder option.
- ◆ A shared folder's permissions can be defined to grant or restrict access to the share in much the same manner as for direct file and folder access. There are only three standard share permissions: Full Control, Change, and Read. You grant them on a user or group basis and can specify either Allow or Deny.
- ◆ A Deny setting always overrides or trumps any Allow setting, even across group memberships for the same share.
- ◆ A user's effective permissions on a resource when accessed through a share are calculated by taking the most restrictive result of the comparison between the cumulative share permissions and the cumulative file-level NTFS permissions.
- ◆ On workgroup member Windows XP clients, you create shared folders in the same manner as you do domain clients, or you can take advantage of Simple File Sharing. Simple File Sharing shares specified folders so that all workgroup users have anonymous access to the shared material. You can indicate at the time of sharing whether to allow network users to change the shared files or not (Change access is enabled by default). To employ Simple File Sharing, drag and drop a folder to be shared into the Shared Documents folder within My Computer or Windows Explorer. To terminate a share from Simple File Sharing, delete the folder name from the Shared Documents folder. Simple File Sharing does not offer any further security controls on shared folders.

OBJECTIVES ON THE JOB

It is important to plan your shares. Create shares to grant groups of users access to resources for which they all have the same file level access permissions. Security should be managed through file-level access permissions, not through share permissions.

PRACTICE TEST QUESTIONS

1. What standard permission manages access for shares on Windows XP Professional? (Choose all that apply.)
   a. Full Control
   b. Read
   c. Read and Modify
   d. Change

2. When Simple File Sharing is enabled on a workgroup system, what type of access is enabled by default?
   a. Full Control to Everyone
   b. Change access to Everyone
   c. Read only access to Everyone
   d. Full Control to the Domain Users group

3. Effective resource permissions are determined by:
   a. calculating the most restrictive share permissions
   b. calculating the most restrictive NTFS permissions
   c. comparing share and NTFS permissions and using the most restrictive
   d. comparing share and NTFS permissions and using the most permissive

4. When a Windows XP Professional system is a member of a domain, a folder can be quickly shared by dragging and dropping the folder into the Shared Documents folder.
   a. True
   b. False

5. When a Windows XP Professional system is a workgroup member, a folder can be shared by accessing the Shared tab of the folder's Properties dialog box and marking the Share this folder radio button.
   a. True
   b. False

6. Both Simple File Sharing and normal network sharing allow you to fine-tune share-level permissions.
   a. True
   b. False

7. Which of the following is true about newly created shares? (Choose all that apply.)
   a. They are set to Full Control to the Everyone group
   b. They are set to Change to the Everyone group
   c. They are set to maximum allowed users
   d. They are set to allow only 16 simultaneous users

OBJECTIVES

2.2.1 Manage and troubleshoot Web server resources

WEB RESOURCE MANAGEMENT

UNDERSTANDING THE OBJECTIVE

Managing Web resources requires knowledge of NTFS file permissions, directory structure, and IIS controls.

WHAT YOU REALLY NEED TO KNOW

- Web resources are simply files and folders placed within a specified directory structure that the **IIS** Web server allows visitors to access.
- Web access can be anonymous or controlled using accounts and passwords. Anonymous access files can be seen by anyone. Only those who provide a valid user name and password can access controlled files.
- IIS uses the ..\inetpub\wwwroot\ directory (as known as Web root) as the location for Web-accessible files for its default Web site. You can create other Web sites with other Web roots, or link to folders anywhere on the network from within an existing Web root.
- The most secure Web root configuration does not link to external folders; a backup of all files and folders within the Web root is actively maintained. Within the Web root, place only those files that you want to grant access to the public or the specific authorized users.
- Access control is managed both on an NTFS level and through IIS. NTFS access permissions function the same as on a non-Web basis. However, anonymous Web access is controlled through a common user account named IUSR_<*IISservername*>. This account should have at least Read access on all files within the Web root that you want the general public to access. All data files anywhere else on the network or local system should not use this account to define access.
- IIS-level access controls are defined on a Web site or subfolder basis. Controls are located on the Directory or Home Directory tab. The check box controls are Script source access (execute), Read, Write, and Directory browsing. In addition to these share-like controls, IIS also offers the ability to block communications from specific IP addresses or domain names (see Objective 6.4).
- If a user has trouble accessing a Web resource, the following actions should resolve the issue: First, make sure the IIS server is running. Then check that the desired resource is correctly located in the Web root path and that the resource's NTFS permissions are properly defined (with the IUSR account or specific users/groups, for example). Verify that the user is connecting to the correct Web server. Finally, verify that IIS is configured to allow access to the resource.

OBJECTIVES ON THE JOB

Managing Web resources takes planning and careful implementation, just as when managing normal network shares.

PRACTICE TEST QUESTIONS

1. Web resources are simply files and folders placed within a specified directory structure, which the IIS Web server allows visitors to access.
    a. True
    b. False

2. Anonymous Web access is more specifically defined as:
    a. unrestricted access to all visitors
    b. access controlled through a common user account
    c. accessing an unknown Web server
    d. logging on to a Web server with a user name but not a password

3. The default directory for the default Web site on Windows XP Professional IIS is:
    a. \WINDOWS\wwwroot
    b. \Program Files\wwwroot
    c. \inetpud\wwwroot\
    d. \Desktop\wwwroot\

4. To grant anonymous visitors access to resources on a Web server, you must assign what type of permission?
    a. Full Control
    b. Change
    c. Read
    d. Web Access Only

5. The primary means by which security is maintained and controlled for a Web server is:
    a. the IIS Web server itself
    b. share-level permissions
    c. NTFS permissions
    d. IPSec

6. The IIS Web server offers site- and folder-level access controls, such as Read, Write, Directory Browsing, and Execute.
    a. True
    b. False

7. A common error that can cause problems when attempting to access a resource through a Web server is:
    a. not being a member of the Domain Users group
    b. using FAT partitions to host the Web root
    c. using a public-leased IP address for the Web server
    d. placing the resource outside the Web root folder

OBJECTIVES

2.3 Connect to local and network print devices; connect to a local print device

LOCAL AND NETWORK PRINTERS

UNDERSTANDING THE OBJECTIVE

Except for files, printers are the most commonly shared resource on a network. Windows XP Professional supports the use of locally attached printers, connecting to printers on other systems on the network, and connecting to network-attached printers.

WHAT YOU REALLY NEED TO KNOW

- Printers are configured through the Printers and Faxes utility. This is found on the Start menu and within Control Panel.
- To connect to a local printer, physically attach the printer to your computer with a parallel, serial, or **USB** cable, then power on the printer. Infrared printers must be oriented properly with the **IR** port on the computer system. Use the Add Printer Wizard (Printers and Faxes utility) to attempt automatic detection. If the printer is not found, you must provide details about its make and model, connected port, printer name, whether to share the printer and its share name, and whether to print a test page.
- To connect to a network printer, use the Add Printer Wizard. Select the A network printer, or A printer attached to another computer option. Select the printer through Active Directory, a **UNC** name, or a **URL** for an Internet printer (see Objective 2.3.3).
- You do not have to install a networked printer to use it. Dragging and dropping a document onto the share name of a printer within My Computer or Windows Explorer will print the document. To print a document, you can also drop it onto the printer name within the Printers and Faxes folder.
- Connecting to network-attached printers typically requires an installation routine provided by the printer's manufacturer. In most cases, the installation routine creates a unique communication port, using a TCP/IP address or a proprietary printer protocol link. The installation routine either completes the printer installation or requires you to use the Add Printer Wizard to complete the installation. Typically, you complete the installation by selecting to install a local printer, and then selecting the custom connection port. After a network-attached printer is installed on one system, that system acts as the printer's print server. All other clients on the network can submit print jobs to the network-attached printer by mapping to the printer share from the print server.
- You must be an administrator to install printers.

OBJECTIVES ON THE JOB

Printing under Windows XP Professional is exactly like printing under Windows 2000. It is easy and straightforward. If a problem occurs, it is caused by a physical connection, by the printer being offline/out of paper/out of ink or toner, or by a corrupted printer drive or share definition. Physical problems must be addressed to return the printer to normal operation. When a driver or share problem occurs, delete the printer definition and then re-create it.

PRACTICE TEST QUESTIONS

1. **Connecting to a local printer requires:**
   a. a network IP address for the printer
   b. a port connection
   c. the DLC protocol
   d. domain membership

2. **When connecting to a network printer, what three methods can be used to locate the printer?**
   a. UNC
   b. DNS
   c. URL
   d. Active Directory

3. **It is possible to share a printer during the installation procedure.**
   a. True
   b. False

4. **What method is available to print a document? (Choose all that apply.)**
   a. Use the print command within an application.
   b. Use the Send To Device command from the File menu.
   c. Drag and drop a document onto a printer share within My Computer.
   d. Drag and drop a document onto the printer name in the Printers and Faxes folder.

5. **A network-attached printer requires a printer server.**
   a. True
   b. False

6. **Who can install printers?**
   a. Any user
   b. Only domain users
   c. Administrators
   d. Guests

7. **What means is used to connect printers to a local system? (Choose all that apply.)**
   a. USB
   b. Infrared
   c. Stereo RCA cable
   d. Parallel cable
   e. Serial cable

OBJECTIVES

2.3.1 Manage printers and print jobs

PRINTER MANAGEMENT

UNDERSTANDING THE OBJECTIVE

Printers are managed through the Printers and Faxes folder. Print jobs are managed through a printer's print queue window.

WHAT YOU REALLY NEED TO KNOW

- Printer management consists of setting a printer's parameters and access permissions (see Objective 2.3.2) through the Properties dialog box for the printer.
- Printer options include portrait and landscape orientation, printing front to back or back to front, printing multiple sheets per page, and selecting the paper tray source.
- Printers can be shared with the network or restricted to local use. A shared printer can store printer drivers for Windows 2000, Windows NT 4.0, Windows 98, Windows Me, and Windows 95 on its print server. When printers are shared, clients do not have to store a printer drive locally, and the driver update process is easier because the drivers are in one location.
- Multiple logical printers can be defined for a single physical print device.
- Advanced settings include defining a restricted print time, defining a priority, and setting spooler options. A printer with restricted print times accepts new print jobs but sends them to the printer only during the prescribed time period. A printer with a higher priority (up to 99) prints to a printer before a printer with a lower priority (down to 1). Spool settings include spool but print immediately, spool but print only after spooling is completed, or don't spool but print directly to printer. The latter setting usually delays the application in returning to user control. Other advanced settings can retain documents that have mismatched document and printer settings, print spooled documents first, and retain all printed documents in spool.
- Print jobs are managed through the print queue. This window displays all print jobs sent to the printer by local or remote users that have not yet been fully sent to the printer. While a print job is displayed in the print queue, it has not begun printing and can be paused, restarted, or deleted. Through the Properties of a print job you can alter the notification user/group, change its priority, and restrict its print times.
- You can manage your own print jobs at any time. Managing other print jobs requires Manage Printers or Manage Documents permission on the printer.
- After stopping a printing job, the printer may continue to print because the stop/pause/delete controls affect only those print jobs still in the print queue. Any portion of a print job already sent to the printer will continue to print.

OBJECTIVES ON THE JOB

It is common practice to define multiple logical printers for a single physical printer, define unique priority and print times for each logical printer, and then assign user and group access to logical printers as needed.

PRACTICE TEST QUESTIONS

1. Printer management can be performed using which tool?
    a. My Computer
    b. Printers and Faxes
    c. System applet
    d. Network Connections

2. A Windows XP Professional print server can host printer drivers for which other operating system? (Choose all that apply.)
    a. Windows 2000
    b. Windows NT 3.51
    c. Windows Me
    d. Windows 95

3. Storing operating system printer drivers on the print server still requires that updated printer drivers be installed on the print server and all clients.
    a. True
    b. False

4. A single physical printer can have several logical printers defined, each with different settings.
    a. True
    b. False

5. Deleting a print job that is partially printed instantly removes it from the print queue and stops the printer from printing additional pages.
    a. True
    b. False

6. A color laser printer in an office has three logical printers defined. One is named ManagerPrnt and has a priority of 99; a second is named OfficePrnt and has a priority of 1; and a third is named ReportPrnt and has a time restriction of 8:00 p.m. to 6:00 a.m. One evening, several staff members are working late on a major project. At 10:30 p.m. three different documents are sent to the color laser printer. All logical printers are configured to print only after the entire print job is spooled. Which document prints first?
    a. The one sent via ManagerPrnt
    b. The one sent via OfficePrnt
    c. The one sent via ReportPrnt
    d. The one with the earliest timestamp

7. If you need to terminate the printing of a confidential document that you accidentally sent to the public office printer, which of the following actions results in the least amount of output on that printer?
    a. Pause the entire print queue.
    b. Pause the selected document from the print queue.
    c. Cancel the selected document in the print queue.
    d. None of the above.

OBJECTIVES

2.3.2 Control access to printers by using permissions

PRINTER ACCESS PERMISSIONS

UNDERSTANDING THE OBJECTIVE

Access to printers is controlled by object permissions in the same manner as files and folders are controlled on NTFS volumes.

WHAT YOU REALLY NEED TO KNOW

- Local printers and network printers are access controlled in the same manner.
- You can define multiple access permission levels for each logical printer.
- You define access permissions for individual users or groups. There are four standard permissions on printers: Print, Manage Printers, Manage Documents, and Special Permissions. You can set each permission for Allow or Deny for each user/group. There is no Full Control permission for printers.
- Print allows users to submit print jobs to the printer and manage their own print jobs.
- Manage Documents allows users to manage any print job in the queue and change permission settings on the printer. It does not grant users the ability to submit print jobs.
- Manage Printers allows users to submit print jobs, and change printer settings, drivers, and permissions. It does not grant users the ability to manage print jobs in the queue.
- Special Permissions are custom permissions defined by selecting from the advanced permissions of Print, Manage Printers, Manage Documents, Read permissions, Change permissions, and Take Ownership.
- The effective permissions for a user on a printer are calculated by adding all granted permissions to that specific user account or their group memberships.
- As with file permissions, a Deny setting always overrides any Allow.

OBJECTIVES ON THE JOB

Controlling access permission over printers is nearly as important as managing file access permission. Users should be given only enough access to perform their specific work requirements. Grant a few select people the Manage Documents or Manage Printers permissions. Granting these permissions to the wrong people may result in deleted print jobs, installation of corrupt drivers, or improper configuration of printers.

PRACTICE TEST QUESTIONS

1. Which permission level is available for printers? (Choose all that apply.)
    a. Print
    b. Manage Documents
    c. Manage Printers
    d. Full Control

2. Which permission level can submit print jobs? (Choose all that apply.)
    a. Print
    b. Manage Documents
    c. Manage Printers
    d. Full Control

3. Which permission level can change access permissions? (Choose all that apply.)
    a. Print
    b. Manage Documents
    c. Manage Printers
    d. Full Control

4. Which permission level grants the ability to manage any print job in the queue?
    a. Print
    b. Manage Documents
    c. Manage Printers
    d. Full Control

5. Bob is a member of the Sales, Report, and Management groups on the network. The Sales group is assigned Print permissions on the CorpLaser printer. The Report group has no assigned permissions on the CorpLaser printer. The Management group is assigned Manage Documents permissions on the CorpLaser printer. What actions can Bob take? (Choose all that apply.)
    a. Submit print jobs.
    b. Change printer permissions.
    c. Change printer priority.
    d. Alter the printer time period for his own print jobs.

6. A recent company audit showed that the CorpLaser printer's permissions were incorrect. To correct the permissions, the Report group was given a Deny setting for Manage Documents. All other settings are the same as in Question 5. What action is Bob now restricted from taking? (Choose all that apply.)
    a. Submit print jobs.
    b. Change printer permissions.
    c. Delete any print job.
    d. Update printer driver.

7. Local printers and network printers are access controlled using different permissions.
    a. True
    b. False

OBJECTIVES

2.3.3 Connect to an Internet printer

INTERNET PRINTING

UNDERSTANDING THE OBJECTIVE

Window XP Professional supports Internet printing. This includes connecting to a printer shared over a Web server or sharing a local printer over IIS from a client system.

WHAT YOU REALLY NEED TO KNOW

- ◆ The Internet printing system supported by Windows XP is made possible by **IPP**. Internet or Web printing (sharing a printer over the Internet) is only possible when the print server is also running IIS. Any client with IPP can connect to an Internet printer hosted by Windows XP.
- ◆ Internet printing allows remote users to submit print jobs, view and manage print queues, and download updated printer drivers.
- ◆ To configure a connection to an Internet printer, use the Add Printer Wizard. Provide the URL for the printer in the form: http://<*printservername*>/printers/<*printersharename*>/.printer. You may need to provide a user name and password with access to the printer. This creates a logical printer that can be used to print documents just like a local or normal network printer.
- ◆ After connecting to the Internet printer and submitting a print job, you can view the print queue by accessing the URL: http://<*printerservername*>/printer/. This displays a list of printers. Selecting a printer displays its print queue and a list of commands you can perform on the queue. The same controls are available through Web queue management as with normal print queues.

OBJECTIVES ON THE JOB

Using Internet printing is an excellent way to provide print services for telecommuters, remote operators, or any type of Internet or intranet client. Internet printing expands the capabilities of Windows XP printing beyond the restrictions of a normal domain or workgroup network. However, be careful to assign print access only as needed and never grant untrusted remote operators Manage Documents or Manage Printers permissions.

PRACTICE TEST QUESTIONS

1. What is the syntax of the URL used to install a local logical printer for an Internet printer?
    a. http://<printservername>/printersharename>/.printer
    b. http://<printservername>/printers
    c. http://<printservername>/printers/.printer
    d. http://<printservername>/printers/<printersharename>/.printer

2. To share a printer through the Web, Windows XP must have what component(s)? (Choose all that apply.)
    a. SSL
    b. IIS
    c. IPP
    d. IPSec

3. Through Internet printing, remote users are able to: (Choose all that apply.)
    a. submit print jobs
    b. view the print queue
    c. change permissions
    d. manage their print jobs
    e. change the printer drivers on the print server

4. To access the print queue over a Web server, what is the syntax of the URL?
    a. http://<printservername>/<printersharename>/.printer
    b. http://<printservername>/printers
    c. http://<printservername>/printers/.printer
    d. http://<printservername>/printers/<printersharename>/.printer

5. Even after you create a logical printer for an Internet printer, you must still print all documents through Internet Explorer.
    a. True
    b. False

6. Internet Printers can be accessed only by Windows XP systems.
    a. True
    b. False

7. The print queue management controls accessed through the Web only include Delete Print Jobs and Properties.
    a. True
    b. False

OBJECTIVES

2.4 Configure and manage file systems; convert from one file system to another file system; configure NTFS, FAT32, or FAT file systems

MANAGING FILE SYSTEMS • NTFS, FAT32, AND FAT • CONVERSION • DEFRAGMENTATION • ERROR CHECKING • DISK CLEANUP

UNDERSTANDING THE OBJECTIVE

Managing Windows XP Professional file systems includes formatting, conversion, defragmentation, error checking, and Disk Cleanup.

WHAT YOU REALLY NEED TO KNOW

- Volumes can be formatted with NTFS, FAT32, or FAT. FAT is used when security is not required and the volume is less than 4 GB. FAT32 is used when security is not required and the volume is 4 GB or larger. NTFS is used when security is important on any volume size. After a volume is formatted, no additional configuration settings are necessary for that volume related to its file system.

- Converting from FAT or FAT32 to NTFS requires the use of the CONVERT command-line utility. All existing data on the volume is retained. Before converting from NTFS to FAT or FAT32, back up the data on the volume and restore it after the volume is formatted.

- Fragmentation occurs when a file is written to a volume in multiple parts and stored in various locations because there is not sufficient contiguous space to store the file in a single location. Defragmented volumes operate faster than fragmented volumes.

- Error checking scans a volume for bad sectors (a physical defect) or broken file chains (such as orphaned fragments of a file). Bad sectors are marked so those areas will not be used. Orphaned file segments are copied into files in the root of the volume (with incremental filenames such as File0001.txt) to allow for possible data extraction.

- Disk Cleanup scans a volume for temporary files, unnecessary downloaded files, unused files for compression, removal of software installations, and so on. Disk Cleanup keeps the clutter on a volume to a minimum. It also enables easy recovery of drive space consumed by useless or unneeded files from various installations or applications and operating systems operations.

OBJECTIVES ON THE JOB

Managing file systems is important to maintain a computer system that is able to efficiently store data, maintain high performance in reading and writing to drives, and maintain the integrity of stored data. You should regularly perform disk cleanup, error checking, and defragmentation on all volumes within your system.

PRACTICE TEST QUESTIONS

1. **Which conversion path results in loss of data on that volume? (Choose all that apply.)**
   a. NTFS to FAT
   b. FAT to NTFS
   c. NTFS to FAT32
   d. FAT32 to NTFS

2. **When converting from FAT32 to NTFS, which of the following steps is required to retain the data stored on that volume?**
   a. Back up the data.
   b. Use the CONVERT utility.
   c. Format the drive through Computer Management.
   d. Restore the data to the volume.

3. **Which file system can be used on a 3 GB volume on a Windows XP Professional system? (Choose all that apply.)**
   a. FAT
   b. FAT32
   c. NTFS

4. **Defragmentation occurs because:**
   a. FAT or FAT32 is used as the file system on the volume
   b. a volume is less than 4 GB in size
   c. the process of writing and deleting files creates a lot of incontiguous space
   d. multiple copies of the same file were stored on a single volume

5. **The error-checking tool locates and manages what type of error? (Choose all that apply.)**
   a. Use of the wrong extension on a file
   b. Physical defects on the drive's surface
   c. Encrypted files whose encryption key has been lost
   d. Orphaned fragments of files

6. **Disk cleanup is used to: (Choose all that apply.)**
   a. reduce the amount of dust collected on a drive
   b. compress files which are rarely used
   c. remove leftover files from application installations
   d. reformat a defragmented drive

7. **Which of the following should be used or performed on a regular basis? (Choose all that apply.)**
   a. Defragment
   b. Error checking
   c. Conversion of file system
   d. Disk Cleanup

OBJECTIVES

2.5 Manage and troubleshoot access to and synchronization of offline files

OFFLINE FILES

UNDERSTANDING THE OBJECTIVE

Offline files store network resources in a local cache so those resources are accessible when not connected to the network. Additionally, even when connected to the network, offline files can provide more efficient access to resources because they are available from the local cache and the data does not have to be accessed and transmitted across the network.

WHAT YOU REALLY NEED TO KNOW

- ♦ When a share is enabled, the caching settings determine whether the files within that share can be stored or cached on remote systems. By default, caching is enabled (Manual caching of documents) but requires that the client manually select files to cache through Offline Files. In addition to the default and disabling caching there are two other options: Automatic caching of documents and Automatic caching of programs and documents. The latter should only be used with read-only data and network-executed applications. Both Automatic options cache resources on the client after the resource is initially accessed.
- ♦ On a client, mark files for use offline by issuing the Make available offline command when you select a file or a folder in My Computer or Windows Explorer.
- ♦ You set offline files configuration settings on the Offline Files tab of the Folder Options applet: Synchronize all offline files when logging on and/or when logging off. Display a reminder every few minutes noting that you are working offline. Create an offline folders shortcut on the desktop. Encrypt offline files to secure data. Set the maximum amount of disk space to be consumed by offline files; view a list of offline files; delete all or specific offline files being stored locally. Note how to handle files when a system goes offline while you are working with a file from that system.
- ♦ The first time a file or folder is marked for offline availability on a client, a wizard starts and enables the offline file service and sets configuration parameters.
- ♦ You force synchronization of offline files by executing the Synchronize Files command from the Tools menu of My Computer or Windows Explorer. You choose which collections of offline files to synchronize. You also access the advanced synchronization settings, such as whether to synchronize automatically upon logon or logoff, only when idle, or at scheduled times.
- ♦ If a problem occurs with offline files, reconnect to the network and force a synchronization. If the problem isn't resolved, remove then remark a file for offline synchronization.

OBJECTIVES ON THE JOB

Offline files should be used only for resources that don't change significantly over time and don't require heightened security to protect them.

PRACTICE TEST QUESTIONS

1. **When a shared resource's cache settings are defined as Automatic caching of documents, what happens?**
    a. Files are pushed to all clients on the network.
    b. Files are cached on all domain controllers to support network load balancing.
    c. Files are retained on clients after they access the share.
    d. Files are marked for caching so they will be retained on all proxy servers.

2. **When a share is created, which of the following is true by default?**
    a. A client automatically caches files from that share when it is accessed.
    b. A client can manually select to cache files from that share.
    c. A client automatically caches files from that share even if it is not accessed.
    d. A client must elect to cache either all network shares or none.

3. **Offline files can be used to make network documents accessible even when disconnected from the network.**
    a. True
    b. False

4. **Files cached locally through offline files are accessed using the same paths as if you were still connected to the network. However, Windows XP offers a configuration setting that places all cached files in a single easy-to-access location.**
    a. True
    b. False

5. **When disconnected from the network, you can delete individual files from a cache.**
    a. True
    b. False

6. **To ensure that your laptop always has the most current version of documents stored locally through offline files, which of the following configuration settings must you enable? (Choose all that apply.)**
    a. Display a reminder every few minutes noting that you are working offline.
    b. Encrypt offline files to secure data.
    c. Synchronize all offline files when logging on.
    d. Synchronize all offline files when logging off.

7. **Synchronization can be set to occur at what time? (Choose all that apply.)**
    a. Logon
    b. Logoff
    c. After a host system has gone offline
    d. After a specified idle time
    e. When cached files reach a specific staleness age
    f. At a specific scheduled time

OBJECTIVES

2.6 Configure and troubleshoot fax support

FAX SUPPORT

UNDERSTANDING THE OBJECTIVE
Windows XP boasts native support for faxing. It requires an HCL-compliant fax modem.

WHAT YOU REALLY NEED TO KNOW

- Fax support within Windows XP is made possible by integrating fax modem controls with the printing subsystem. Once faxing is configured, you fax documents using the same process as printing, except you select the fax as the printer. Faxing is not enabled by default.
- The Printers and Faxes tool is used to install and configure faxing. Click the Set up faxing command in the quick list to install the necessary components and enable faxing. Once completed, a fax icon appears alongside installed printers icons.
- Faxing is configured through the Properties dialog box of the fax icon. Settings include paper size, image quality, orientation, access permissions, **TSID**, **CSID**, call retries, retry delay, restrict faxing to time periods, auto answer on ring count or manual answer, print on receipt, save to folder on receipt, notification options, and fax archiving.
- Fax devices cannot be shared on a network under the Windows XP native fax service.
- Fax devices have two security tabs: Security and Fax Security. The Security tab controls fax access like a printer using the Print, Manage Printers, and Manage Documents permissions. The Fax Security tab manages fax services with Fax, Manage Fax Configuration, and Manage Fax Documents.
- The Fax Console is used like a normal printer queue, but offers details about incoming faxes, received faxes, outgoing faxes, and sent faxes. From this interface you can view, delete, save a copy, forward through e-mail, and print a fax. The Fax Console can be accessed by double-clicking a Fax icon or through the Start menu.
- The Fax Monitor displays the current activity of a fax in progress. This interface can be used to answer an incoming fax or to terminate an outgoing fax.
- A fax modem configured to answer incoming faxes cannot be used to answer incoming dial-up connections.
- If faxing fails, check that the fax modem is properly installed, the phone lines are securely connected, and that the correct driver is installed. If faxing continues to fail, delete the fax from the Printers and Faxes window and re-create it. Note that this deletes items in the Fax Console, but does not alter faxes archived to disk.

OBJECTIVES ON THE JOB
Faxing from the desktop reduces paper waste by eliminating the need to print a document on paper before faxing. Likewise, receiving faxes as digital documents allows more efficient storage and forwarding of documents without using paper or requiring scanning.

PRACTICE TEST QUESTIONS

1. Faxing is enabled and controlled through:
   a. Computer Management
   b. the same interface as printing
   c. System applet
   d. My Computer

2. Faxing is fully installed and ready for use by default when a typical installation of Windows XP Professional is performed.
   a. True
   b. False

3. Fax devices under Windows XP Professional native support can be shared on a network.
   a. True
   b. False

4. Which of the following statements is true about the Fax Console? (Choose all that apply.)
   a. It acts as the print queue for faxing.
   b. It allows a user to delete a fax job, even before it has been sent.
   c. It allows a user to alter the destination phone number of a fax job before it is sent.
   d. It allows a user to view the content of a fax.
   e. It allows a user to e-mail a fax document.

5. Which of the following is a valid configuration option of Windows XP faxing? (Choose all that apply.)
   a. Automatic answer on ring count
   b. Refuse answer from specific phone numbers or area codes
   c. Print on receipt
   d. Save fax to a file

6. If you cannot or are unable to initiate a receive action for an incoming fax, which of the following is a valid way to troubleshoot this problem? (Choose all that apply.)
   a. Check the modem driver.
   b. Verify that the modem is not set to answer incoming dial-up connections.
   c. Update your proxy settings.
   d. Reseat the phone cable.
   e. Reinstall Windows XP.

7. Deleting a fax from the Printer and Faxes window also clears out the Fax Console and all archived faxes.
   a. True
   b. False

Section 3

Implementing, Managing, Monitoring, and Troubleshooting Hardware Devices and Drivers

OBJECTIVES

3.1 Implement, manage, and troubleshoot disk devices; monitor and configure disks; monitor, configure, and troubleshoot volumes

DISK DEVICE MANAGEMENT

UNDERSTANDING THE OBJECTIVE

Hard drives are an integral part of computer systems. A hard drive is required in most cases, and especially with Windows XP, to store the operating system and local data files. Understanding how to work with hard drives is an important aspect of system administration.

WHAT YOU REALLY NEED TO KNOW

- You manage disk devices primarily with the Disk Management tool found within the Computer Management tool.
- Implementing a disk device requires that it be physically installed and its drivers installed (manually through Add Hardware, or automatically through Plug and Play).
- A used drive (marked as foreign in the drive listing within Disk Management) must be imported using the Import Foreign Disk command. Existing partitions are retained and FAT, FAT32, or NTFS volumes are assigned drive letters.
- New drives must be partitioned/volumed and formatted. Once formatted, drive letters are automatically assigned.
- Using the Disk Management tool, you can perform the following on drives: partition/volume, format, convert to basic or dynamic drives, assign drive letters or paths (mount points), and mark as active. Through a drive's properties, you can enable/disable write caching and perform driver management. Driver management includes updating, rolling back, or uninstalling the device driver.
- Troubleshooting drive problems can involve rescanning the system's drives, restarting, reformatting, repartitioning, and replacing the physical drive and starting over.
- When converting from basic to dynamic storage, all drive divisions (called partitions in basic storage) are retained as volumes (as they are labeled in dynamic storage). All data is retained. When converting from dynamic to basic, all data is lost. Thus, to retain stored data, you must perform a backup before reverting to basic.
- The properties of a partition/volume can be used to access and start Disk Cleanup, defragmentation, error checking, and back up. The Help and Support Troubleshooter walks you through plausible solutions for common problems related to drives.
- Drives as a whole can be monitored through System Monitor by viewing the PhysicalDisk object counters. Volumes and partitions can be monitored by viewing the LogicalDisk object counters.

OBJECTIVES ON THE JOB

If a hard drive presents problems, you should try error checking, reformatting, and/or repartitioning before replacing the hard drive. However, the more a hard drive is used, the more likely the chance of failure. Consider replacing active hard drives every three years.

PRACTICE TEST QUESTIONS

1. A new hard drive, once physically installed in a computer, is instantly available to store data.
    a. True
    b. False

2. After a drive is formatted, you must manually assign a drive letter.
    a. True
    b. False

3. New partitions can be created using which tool?
    a. Windows Explorer
    b. My Computer
    c. System Monitor
    d. Computer Management

4. Disk Cleanup, defragmentation, error checking, and back up can be launched directly through which interface?
    a. Computer Management
    b. A drive's Properties dialog box
    c. System applet
    d. Network Monitor

5. Counters found in the PhysicalDisk object in System Monitor are used to view performance measurements for:
    a. virtual memory usage
    b. hard drives as a whole
    c. individual volumes or partitions
    d. CPU cache interrupts

6. What steps should be taken to troubleshoot a disk drive that is no longer functioning properly? (Choose all that apply.)
    a. Restart
    b. Reformat
    c. Repartition
    d. all of the above

7. When converting from dynamic to basic storage, what action must be taken to ensure data retention?
    a. Use the convert tool with the /e parameter.
    b. Use FSUTIL to convert the drive.
    c. Back up data before reverting to basic storage.
    d. No additional precautions are necessary, converting to basic storage retains all data stored on the drive.

OBJECTIVES

3.1.1 Install, configure, and manage DVD and CD-ROM devices

DVD AND CD-ROM DEVICES

UNDERSTANDING THE OBJECTIVE

CD and DVD devices are managed through the Disk Management tool and the Properties dialog boxes of My Computer/Windows Explorer. DVD and CD-ROM management is similar to management of hard drives.

WHAT YOU REALLY NEED TO KNOW

- To install DVD and CD-ROM devices, you must install the physical devices and the drivers. Drivers are usually installed automatically through Plug and Play, but manual installation using Add Hardware or a vendor installation disk is also common.
- With basic drivers, Windows XP should be able to access the data on a normal data or audio CD from either a DVD or CD-ROM drive.
- For DVD movie playback, you must purchase and install a DVD decoder. This can be a hardware device or a software product. Windows XP is not equipped with a native DVD decoder. Windows XP also does not have the native ability to write DVDs to a DVD burner.
- Data and audio can be burned to **CD-Rs** and **CD-RWs** if you have a CD-R or CD-RW drive. Windows XP natively supports CD-R/CD-RW burning.
- To manage a CD or DVD drive through Disk Management, you enable/disable the device for a hardware profile, start the troubleshooter, set internal playback volume, enable/disable digital CD audio, perform driver management (update, roll back, and uninstall), and change the drive letter.
- Through the Properties dialog box for My Computer or Windows Explorer, you can configure the AutoPlay and share settings. For each of the five basic CD types (music files, pictures, video files, mixed content, and music), you can select an AutoPlay action. Options include: prompt each time (default), play, open, no action, print, view slideshow, or copy pictures to a folder (the later three apply only to picture file CDs).
- The method used for sharing a CD or DVD drive is the same as any drive or folder sharing. You elect to share it, define a share name, elect unlimited or a specific number of simultaneous users, define the access permissions for users and groups, and set caching options.

OBJECTIVES ON THE JOB

CD burners are becoming a commonplace peripheral on home and office computers. CDs can be convenient for moving and storing large collections of data; however, they can pose a security risk by allowing data to be easily copied off a system. The presence and supervision of CD burners in an office environment should be addressed in an organization's security policy.

PRACTICE TEST QUESTIONS

1. **How are CD and DVD drives typically installed? (Choose all that apply.)**
    a. Automatically through Plug and Play
    b. Using the CD Device applet
    c. Using a vendor-supplied installation disk
    d. Manually through Add Hardware

2. **Windows XP supports which of the following activities natively? (Choose all that apply.)**
    a. CD data disk read
    b. CD audio disk playback
    c. DVD playback
    d. CD-R/CD-RW burning

3. **Windows XP can burn data CDs but not audio CDs natively.**
    a. True
    b. False

4. **It is not possible to change the drive letter of a CD-ROM drive.**
    a. True
    b. False

5. **What is the default setting for the Window XP CD AutoPlay feature?**
    a. Launch slideshow for picture CDs
    b. AutoPlay for audio CDs
    c. AutoPlay for video file CDs
    d. Prompt for action on mixed CDs

6. **Shared CD or DVD drives do not allow user limitations or offer caching controls.**
    a. True
    b. False

7. **CD and DVD management may include: (Choose all that apply.)**
    a. disabling the device in a hardware profile
    b. setting internal playback volume
    c. partitioning the media
    d. rolling back the driver
    e. converting from basic to dynamic storage
    f. enabling digital CD audio
    g. importing foreign drives

OBJECTIVES

3.1.2 Monitor and configure removable media, such as tape devices

REMOVABLE MEDIA

UNDERSTANDING THE OBJECTIVE

Windows XP supports removable media. Ranging from floppies to pull-out hard drives, removable media offer numerous options for transporting data.

WHAT YOU REALLY NEED TO KNOW

- Removable media can contain only a single primary partition.
- Removable media cannot participate in dynamic storage.
- Removable media cannot host extended partitions.
- Removable media cannot be marked active.
- Removable media are managed through the Removable Storage section of Computer Management. Removable Storage is used to track removable media and catalog the media libraries used by automated robotic media devices (such as changers and jukeboxes) and manually operated media devices (such as CD-R/CD-RW drives and tape drives). A media library is any collection of storage media for a read/write device. A media pool is a subset of the library of storage media for a specific device.
- Before its first use, you should clean/format new media using the Cleaner Management Wizard.
- To prevent performance degradation, limit the total size of all media libraries managed on a single system to less than 1000 media elements.
- Access permissions can be assigned to removable storage to prevent unauthorized user access. Permissions are Use, Control, and Modify, which are assigned on a user or group basis with an Allow or Deny setting.
- Configuring removable media through Removable Storage involves creating media pools, inserting and ejecting media through libraries, mounting and dismounting media, viewing the status of media and libraries, cleaning media, performing library inventories, and setting access security.

OBJECTIVES ON THE JOB

Removable storage management offers a means by which the complicated storage history of a backup device or a CD-R/CD-RW can be easily tracked. Through Removable Storage, you can easily locate specific media on which desired files are stored.

PRACTICE TEST QUESTIONS

1. What is the maximum recommended total of media elements present across all libraries on a single system?
    a. 150
    b. 1000
    c. 2048
    d. 16,512

2. What type of access permission control is available on removable media through Removable Storage? (Choose all that apply.)
    a. Full Control
    b. Read
    c. Use
    d. Write
    e. Control
    f. Read & Execute
    g. Modify

3. Which of the following is true?
    a. Removable media can contain only a single primary partition.
    b. Removable media can participate in dynamic storage.
    c. Removable media can host extended partitions.
    d. Removable media can be marked active.

4. Any collection of storage media for a read/write device is a:
    a. media pool
    b. drive set
    c. media library
    d. data set

5. New media should be cleaned/formatted through the Cleaner Management Wizard before its first use.
    a. True
    b. False

6. Which of the following is a valid action or function possible through Removable Storage? (Choose all that apply.)
    a. Create media pools
    b. Partition media
    c. Insert and eject media through libraries
    d. Mount and dismount media
    e. Import foreign media
    f. View the status of media and libraries
    g. Clean media
    h. Convert to dynamic media
    i. Perform library inventories

OBJECTIVES

3.2 Implement, manage, and troubleshoot display devices; install, configure, and troubleshoot a video adapter

VIDEO ADAPTER

UNDERSTANDING THE OBJECTIVE

Managing video adapters primarily involves driver issues and configuration settings.

WHAT YOU REALLY NEED TO KNOW

- Windows XP requires an SVGA 800 x 600 video adapter for installation.
- Changing video adapters requires reverting to the minimum supported resolution and color depth, then physically removing the old adapter and installing the new adapter. Upon startup, the operating system attempts a Plug and Play detection and installation of the model-specific drivers. If Plug and Play fails to detect the new adapter and install the proper drivers, use Add Hardware or a vendor-provided installation disk.
- You set screen resolution and color quality on the Settings tab of the Display applet. The Advanced button opens the Monitor and Adapter Properties dialog box, from which you can configure the **DPI** setting, configure whether to restart when display changes are made, access video adapter properties, access monitor properties, set screen refresh rate, set hardware acceleration, enable write combining, and install color management profiles.
- Clicking the Troubleshooting button on the Settings tab of the Display applet starts a video- and display-related step-by-step troubleshooting wizard.
- Troubleshooting video problems may involve the following: restarting using Safe Mode, restarting in Normal Mode with VGA enabled, rolling back a video driver, updating a video driver, or replacing the video adapter.
- Through an adapter's properties you can enable or disable the device for a hardware profile, manage the driver, and alter system resources (on some adapters only).
- If the computer stops responding, DirectX applications are failing, on-screen rendering is faulty, the mouse pointer does not move smoothly, or images are corrupted, reduce the hardware acceleration level from Full toward None (there are six level settings).
- If you experience display corruption or other display problems, disable write combining.
- If your display acts sluggish, you should reduce the color quality or resolution. You should also consider disabling some or all of the visual effects. (This is done using the Effects button on the Appearance tab of the Display applet. You also can use the Visual Effects tab of the Performance Options dialog box, accessed through the Performance section's Settings button on the Advanced tab of the System applet.)

OBJECTIVES ON THE JOB

If you have an 8 MB (or higher) video card and are experiencing video/display problems, seek solutions by working with the drivers or the configuration of the adapter. In most cases, you have sufficient memory on the card to handle the display requirements of Windows XP.

PRACTICE TEST QUESTIONS

1. **Which of the following is a reasonable first step in resolving a video display problem? (Choose all that apply.)**
    a. Update the video driver.
    b. Reinstall Windows XP.
    c. Replace the video adapter with a 32 MB adapter.
    d. Reduce the color quality of the display.

2. **Which problem can be resolved by reducing hardware acceleration? (Choose all that apply.)**
    a. DirectX applications are failing.
    b. Your password is not accepted.
    c. On-screen rendering is faulty.
    d. Mouse pointer does not move smoothly.
    e. A service fails during startup.
    f. Images are corrupted.

3. **What troubleshooting step may resolve display corruption?**
    a. Reduce color quality.
    b. Roll back the driver.
    c. Disable write combining.
    d. Increase the resolution.

4. **You are working as a screen capture artist for a publisher. On your current project, nearly every screen shot has a different requirement for screen resolution and color quality. You must make over 100 screen shots for this project. Which of the following settings would make the task more efficient?**
    a. Increase the DPI setting.
    b. Reduce the screen refresh rate.
    c. Disable restart after display changes.
    d. Set hardware acceleration to Full.

5. **What is the minimum video requirement for installing Windows XP?**
    a. VGA 640 x 480
    b. VGA 800 x 600
    c. SVGA 800 x 600
    d. SVGA 1024 x 768

6. **You've just updated the driver for a video adapter. On the next attempted restart, the system displays nothing on the monitor after the initial Windows XP splash screen. What should you do first to restore the system to working order?**
    a. Roll back the video driver.
    b. Start with the Last Known Good Configuration.
    c. Replace the video adapter.
    d. Reduce the level of hardware acceleration.

OBJECTIVES

3.2.1 Configure multiple-display support

MULTIPLE DISPLAYS

UNDERSTANDING THE OBJECTIVE

Windows XP natively supports up to 10 display devices. This means multiple monitors (multiple displays) can be used to display a greatly expanded desktop.

WHAT YOU REALLY NEED TO KNOW

- When multiple monitors are used, each monitor is controlled by its own video adapter. Some video adapters with two or more connection heads are available, but when configured to support multiple monitors, each adapter head acts like a distinct and separate video adapter.
- Multiple adapters are installed after the initial installation of Windows XP. Additional adapters are installed by physically installing them first, then allowing Plug and Play to detect and install drivers. If necessary, drivers can be manually installed using Add Hardware or an install disk from the vendor. Once installed, multiple monitors are managed from the same Settings tab of the Display applet in Control Panel. To extend the desktop to newly installed monitors, select the new monitor and mark the Extend my Windows desktop onto this monitor check box. The arrangement of the multiple displays is set on this tab by dragging and dropping the monitor icons. The only valid arrangement configurations are rectangles.
- One monitor/adapter set will serve as the primary display. The primary display will show the logon box at startup, and is where all unassigned windows will appear when first opened.
- Any installed adapter can be assigned as the primary display. This is done by selecting a monitor's icon, and then marking the Use this device as the primary monitor check box.
- Application windows and dialog boxes can be dragged across the desktop, and therefore from one monitor to another.
- Dualview is the Windows XP feature that enables a laptop system to display the same desktop on both the built-in **LCD** display and on an external monitor.

OBJECTIVES ON THE JOB

It may take awhile to become accustomed to using multiple monitors. Having a desktop spread out over several monitors can simplify complex work tasks such as graphics design or CAD because a large number of open windows can be viewed simultaneously at a reasonable viewing size.

PRACTICE TEST QUESTIONS

1. Windows XP supports a maximum of how many monitors?
    a. one
    b. two
    c. nine
    d. 10

2. When two or more video adapters are installed in a system, they are managed through what tool?
    a. Multiple Display utility
    b. DualView applet
    c. Display applet
    d. System applet

3. Newly installed additional video adapters automatically extend the desktop.
    a. True
    b. False

4. The primary display must be a video adapter with two or more connection heads.
    a. True
    b. False

5. The Display applet offers settings to specify which monitor a specific application will use as its default initial display area.
    a. True
    b. False

6. Which of the following are valid arrangements of multiple monitors? (Choose all that apply.)
    a. A four-by-four square
    b. A triangle with three levels of three, two, and one monitor(s)
    c. A circle with the primary monitor in the center and eight monitors arranged at N, NE, E, SE, S, SW, W, and NW compass divisions
    d. A rectangle shape of three rows of four monitors
    e. Six monitors arranged in two parallel rows of three

7. Dualview enables simultaneous viewing of a desktop display on a laptop's LCD display and on an external monitor.
    a. True
    b. False

OBJECTIVES

3.3 Configure Advanced Configuration Power Interface (ACPI)

ACPI

UNDERSTANDING THE OBJECTIVE

ACPI power management allows the entire computer—hardware, operating system, and software—to efficiently manage power consumption.

WHAT YOU REALLY NEED TO KNOW

- ACPI is installed by Windows XP during initial installation if all components support power management. If a legacy device is present that does not support power management, it may cause erratic problems when power management is attempted.
- In many cases, **ISA** components and systems with older **BIOS** do not fully support power management.
- Use the Power Options applet to manage all aspects of power management. Power schemes are power profiles that indicate how long to wait before turning off idle monitors or hard drives. Windows XP includes several predefined power schemes that can be customized as needed. A power scheme can also include an idle time to hibernate setting if **APM** is enabled.
- Windows XP supports standby and hibernation. Standby is a low power-consumption mode in which the system state is stored in RAM. You can restore the system by pressing the power button once. However, if battery power fails while in standby, the system state is lost and all unsaved data is lost. Hibernation saves the system state to the hard drive, and then completely powers off. Restoring the system is done in the same manner as a normal restart; however, after logon, the desktop is presented as it was when hibernation was initiated, with all open applications.
- Standby is a feature of ACPI. If ACPI is not present, standby is not offered as a shutdown option.
- If hibernation is enabled but not seen as an option in the Selection dialog box for Shutdown, hold down the Shift key.
- Windows XP supports **UPS** integration; the UPS informs Windows XP of a power loss and Windows XP performs a shutdown prior to total power loss.

OBJECTIVES ON THE JOB

The power management features of Windows XP offer extended battery-based uptime for most portable systems. Defining a custom power scheme to turn off the monitor and hard drives after five minutes greatly extends the life of the battery.

PRACTICE TEST QUESTIONS

1. **ACPI is automatically installed on all computers when Windows XP is installed.**
    a. True
    b. False

2. **Which of the following prevents ACPI from being installed automatically by Windows XP? (Choose all that apply.)**
    a. all devices are ACPI-compliant
    b. not a portable system
    c. ISA devices
    d. older BIOS

3. **A power scheme can be used to define what action? (Choose all that apply.)**
    a. Power off the monitor after a certain number of idle minutes.
    b. Selectively disable power to installed adapters (video, NIC, sound, modem, etc.).
    c. Power off the hard drives after a certain number of idle minutes.
    d. Start automatic system hibernation after a certain number of idle minutes.

4. **Which of the following shutdown mechanisms retains the desktop and all open applications even if the battery is removed from the portable system?**
    a. Standby
    b. Hibernation
    c. Shutdown
    d. Restart

5. **Which of the following shutdown mechanisms restores the system to a usable state in the shortest time?**
    a. Standby
    b. Hibernation
    c. Shutdown
    d. Restart

6. **Which shutdown mechanism is offered only if ACPI is installed?**
    a. Standby
    b. Hibernation
    c. Shutdown
    d. Restart

7. **In the event of a power failure, a Windows XP system with an attached UPS may continue to operate normally for several minutes before automatically shutting down.**
    a. True
    b. False

OBJECTIVES

3.4.1 Implement, manage, and troubleshoot input and output (I/O) devices; monitor, configure, and troubleshoot I/O devices, such as printers, scanners, multimedia devices, mouse, keyboard, and smart card reader; monitor, configure, and troubleshoot multimedia hardware, such as cameras; install, configure, and manage modems; install, configure, and manage Infrared Data Association (IrDA) devices; install, configure, and manage wireless devices; install, configure, and manage USB devices; and install, configure, and manage hand held devices

I/O DEVICE • INSTALLATION • MANAGEMENT

UNDERSTANDING THE OBJECTIVE

I/O devices are any peripheral or adapter cards added to the core components of a computer. I/O devices include printers, scanners, multimedia devices, mice, keyboards, smart card readers, cameras, modems, **IrDA** devices, wireless devices, USB devices, and handheld devices.

WHAT YOU REALLY NEED TO KNOW

- ◆ In most cases, new I/O devices are installed by physically installing or attaching the device, and then starting the system and/or powering up the device. If automatically detected by Windows XP, drivers may be installed without further action by the user. If drivers are not automatically installed, you may need to install them manually through the Add Hardware applet or use a vendor-supplied installation disk.

- ◆ Through Device Manager, you can access a device's Properties dialog box to configure device-specific settings, manage drivers (upgrade, roll back, uninstall), and start a device- or issue-specific troubleshooter.

- ◆ In addition to the Add Hardware applet and Device Manager, which can be used to install and manage all devices, there are some additional Control Panel applets for specific types of devices, such as Keyboard, Mouse, Printers and Faxes, Game Controllers, and Sounds and Audio Devices.

- ◆ You use the Scanners and Cameras applet to manage digital-imaging devices such as scanners, still digital cameras, digital video cameras, and other image-capturing devices. This applet captures images from the device and saves them to a folder, sets device properties, deletes images from the device, and prints images.

- ◆ You use the Phone and Modem Options applet to manage phone and modem devices, define dialing locations, and define how to charge long-distance calls to calling cards.

OBJECTIVES ON THE JOB

A computer's flexibility in function and capability is usually determined by the installed peripherals. Windows XP supports a broad range of I/O devices and connection technologies. Make sure all devices are HCL-compliant before attempting installation. Device drivers for peripherals can cause system and performance problems if they are incompatible with Windows XP.

PRACTICE TEST QUESTIONS

1. Each type of I/O device must be installed using its own dedicated Control Panel applet.
    a. True
    b. False

2. I/O devices can be installed using what method? (Choose all that apply.)
    a. Automatic Plug and Play installation
    b. Device Manager
    c. through the Add Hardware applet
    d. using a vendor-supplied installation disk

3. Distinct Control Panel applets exist for which type of device? (Choose all that apply.)
    a. Faxes
    b. Scanners
    c. Hard drives
    d. Modems
    e. Floppy controllers

4. Through which tool can you access and change the resource settings for a device? (Choose all that apply.)
    a. System Information
    b. Device Manager
    c. Computer Management
    d. Help and Support Center

5. You use the Scanners and Cameras applet to manage only still image digital-capture devices.
    a. True
    b. False

6. Through the Scanners and Cameras applet, you can perform which of the following actions? (Choose all that apply.)
    a. Capture images from the device and save them to a folder.
    b. Set device properties.
    c. Set display properties for viewing images on the monitor.
    d. Delete images from a device.
    e. Print images.

7. Calling card usage is defined through the Phone and Modems applet.
    a. True
    b. False

OBJECTIVES

3.4.2 Implement, manage, and troubleshoot input and output (I/O) devices; monitor, configure, and troubleshoot I/O devices, such as printers, scanners, multimedia devices, mouse, keyboard, and smart card reader; monitor, configure, and troubleshoot multimedia hardware, such as cameras; install, configure, and manage modems; install, configure, and manage Infrared Data Association (IrDA) devices; install, configure, and manage wireless devices; install, configure, and manage USB devices; and install, configure, and manage hand held devices (cont)

I/O DEVICE • INSTALLATION • MANAGEMENT

UNDERSTANDING THE OBJECTIVE

I/O devices are any peripheral or adapter card added to the core components of a computer. This includes printers, scanners, multimedia devices, mice, keyboards, smart card readers, cameras, modems, IrDA devices, wireless devices, USB devices, and handheld devices.

WHAT YOU REALLY NEED TO KNOW

- ♦ IrDA, wireless, and USB devices are installed by orienting them to the computer's IrDA port, placing them within the wireless range of their host computer, making sure signal interference will not prevent communications, or connecting the USB cable respectively, and then powering up the devices. In most cases, the device is detected and installed by Windows XP. If not, restart the system to initiate the detection and installation process. If the device is still not detected, use the Add Hardware applet. Once installed, devices are managed the same way as their direct-connect or adapter card counterparts. Handheld devices are usually IrDA, wireless, or USB devices.

- ♦ Troubleshooting I/O devices typically involves upgrading or rolling back the driver for that device. It that fails to correct the problem, compare the configuration settings to the vendor's recommendations. If you detect a system resource conflict, such as an **IRQ** or memory address conflict, attempt to resolve the conflict by using the Resource tab of the device's Properties dialog box. Disconnecting and reconnecting the device or switching its cable, connector, or bus slot might also resolve the issue. In every case, perform only one change at a time and restart the system, power cycling the device between each attempt. Use the Windows XP Help and Support Center troubleshooter or contact the vendor for additional assistance.

OBJECTIVES ON THE JOB

A computer's flexibility in function and capability is usually determined by the installed peripherals. Windows XP supports a broad range of I/O devices and connection technologies. Make sure all devices are HCL-compliant before attempting installation. Device drivers for peripherals can cause system and performance problems if they are incompatible with Windows XP.

PRACTICE TEST QUESTIONS

1. When properly oriented or connected, which of the following device types are typically detected and installed by Windows XP? (Choose all that apply.)
    a. USB
    b. IrDA
    c. ISA
    d. Wireless

2. Which of the following can prevent a wireless device from being detected by the computer? (Choose all that apply.)
    a. No power to the device
    b. A strong electrical device between the device and the computer
    c. The device not being in the computer's direct line of sight
    d. Power to both the device and the computer from the same wall outlet

3. If a USB device is not detected by Windows XP the moment it is attached, what other option may be available to you to accomplish the installation? (Choose all that apply.)
    a. Add Hardware applet
    b. Restarting the system
    c. Connecting the device with a serial cable
    d. Vendor-supplied installation disk

4. After an IrDA or wireless device is installed, a new Wireless Devices applet appears in Control Panel to manage and configure these devices.
    a. True
    b. False

5. If a device fails to operate after upgrading the driver, what should be done first to restore the device to working order?
    a. Reinstall Windows XP.
    b. Roll back the driver.
    c. Replace the device.
    d. Disable driver signing.

6. If a device is added to a system and its driver installed, but the device fails to work properly, what is the most likely cause of the failure?
    a. User not logged in as an administrator
    b. System resource conflict
    c. Wrong operating system version of the driver
    d. Computer does not meet the minimum requirements of Windows XP

OBJECTIVES

3.5 Manage and troubleshoot drivers and driver signing

DRIVER SIGNING

UNDERSTANDING THE OBJECTIVE

In Windows XP, driver signing prevents corrupted or virus-infected drivers from being installed accidentally.

WHAT YOU REALLY NEED TO KNOW

- A computer administrator defines driver signing. You access the Driver Signing Options dialog box by clicking the Driver Signing button on the Hardware tab of the System applet.
- Driver signing has three settings: Ignore - Install the software anyway and don't ask for my approval; Warn - Prompt me each time to choose an action (default); and Block - Never install unsigned driver software. You can make any of these settings the system default.
- Microsoft recommends using only software that has been digitally signed as Designed for Microsoft Windows XP. Unsigned device drivers can cause system failures and infect the system with a virus.
- If you are unable to install a device driver, check the driver signing settings. If the driver is not signed and Block is selected, you cannot install the device.
- Driver signing relies on the Signature Verification tool (Sigverif) to check drivers before they are installed. This tool can also be used manually to check whether a file is digitally signed. By default, this tool is set to scan only system files located in the main \WINDOWS directory.
- View the log file (Sigverif.txt), created with the Sigverif tool, to see whether drivers and files are signed. By default, the tool records information about all scanned files in the log file.

OBJECTIVES ON THE JOB

Driver signing is a great benefit to administrators because it further restricts the end users' ability to install devices and software. By ensuring that only Microsoft-approved drivers and software are installed, the end user client system will remain stable.

PRACTICE TEST QUESTIONS

1. By default, the driver signing settings of Windows XP prevent any unsigned driver from being installed.
    a. True
    b. False
2. Driver signing can be set to restrict unsigned driver installations for all users of a system.
    a. True
    b. False
3. If you want end users to have the option of installing unsigned drivers but advise them of the possible consequences of doing so, which is the best setting for driver signing?
    a. Ignore
    b. Warn
    c. Block
    d. Enable
4. After installing a new device, your virus-detection tool claims you've been infected with a virus. What is the most likely cause of that infection?
    a. Using a USB device
    b. Being logged on as a computer administrator
    c. Driver signing set to Ignore
    d. Being a domain member
5. If you cannot install a device, what is a possible cause?
    a. You're a computer administrator.
    b. Windows XP meets the minimal system requirements.
    c. Driver signing is set to Block.
    d. There is over 1 GB of free space on the main hard drive.
6. The Sigverif tool can be used to scan device drivers only.
    a. True
    b. False
7. If you suspect an unsigned driver has been installed, how can you locate it?
    a. Review the Sigverif.txt file.
    b. Perform a signature scan with Sigverif.
    c. Perform a signature scan from the Driver Signing Options dialog box.
    d. View the System Information's Software section.

OBJECTIVES

3.6 Monitor and configure multiprocessor computers

MULTIPROCESSORS

UNDERSTANDING THE OBJECTIVE

Windows XP Professional can support up to two processors.

WHAT YOU REALLY NEED TO KNOW

- ◆ To install a second CPU for use by Windows XP, you can either reinstall Windows XP or upgrade the CPU/motherboard driver. The process is as follows: physically install the second CPU and then upgrade the computer driver through Device Manager. (Select the multi-CPU option.)
- ◆ Updating the CPU driver after reverting to a single CPU is accomplished similar to installing a second CPU. The difference is to select Standard PC instead of the multi-CPU system option in Device Manager.
- ◆ The activity of a system's CPU can be tracked through System Monitor's Processor object by selecting the separate instances or the Total instance. The Total instance combines measurements from all CPUs into a single measurement.
- ◆ After a process is active, you can assign it a processor affinity. This is accomplished from the right-click menu of a process on the Task Manager's Processes tab. A list of CPUs appears. Uncheck all CPU check boxes that you want to remain unaffected. Processor affinity is not persistent or sustained across restarts or termination, or by restarting the same process.
- ◆ All CPUs installed in a system must be the exact same make, model, and speed.
- ◆ After a second CPU is installed on a system, you can view a separate CPU utilization graph for each CPU. On Task Manager's Performance tab, click View, and then change the CPU History setting to One Graph Per CPU. You can return to displaying a single graph by changing this setting to One Graph All CPUs.

OBJECTIVES ON THE JOB

Multiple CPUs offer significantly more performance power to a Windows XP system. Setting the affinity for CPU-intensive programs to a second CPU might result in a more efficient operating environment. However, it might also cause system performance to degrade. You should experiment before implementing a second CPU on a production system.

PRACTICE TEST QUESTIONS

1. **Windows XP requires reinstallation if you add a second CPU.**
    a. True
    b. False

2. **The first step in installing a second CPU is to:**
    a. install drivers
    b. start in Safe Mode
    c. physically install the second CPU
    d. reinstall Windows XP

3. **To revert to a single CPU after a second CPU has been in use requires a reinstallation of Windows XP.**
    a. True
    b. False

4. **Monitoring the activity of multiple CPUs requires the use of:**
    a. the System applet
    b. the System Monitor
    c. the Network applet
    d. the System Information

5. **Processor affinity is persistent across restarts.**
    a. True
    b. False

6. **Setting the processor affinity for an application with high-CPU requirements to a second CPU always improves performance.**
    a. True
    b. False

7. **Task Manager can display a history graph for each CPU and for each section of RAM used by each CPU.**
    a. True
    b. False

Section 4

Monitoring and Optimizing System Performance and Reliability

OBJECTIVES

4.1 Monitor, optimize, and troubleshoot performance of the Windows XP Professional desktop

DESKTOP MANAGEMENT

UNDERSTANDING THE OBJECTIVE

Optimizing the desktop focuses on maximizing the speed at which Windows XP responds to user input. This involves tuning the various subsystems and monitoring the activity of those subsystems.

WHAT YOU REALLY NEED TO KNOW

- Every Windows XP object's performance can be monitored and measured through System Monitor.
- System Monitor can view measurement data from local and remote machines in real time or from a log file. In addition to recording log files, System Monitor can also issue custom performance alerts to indicate when a performance metric has crossed a defined threshold. (See Objectives 4.1.1–4.1.4 for details.)
- Task Manager is a useful tool for monitoring performance. The Performance tab displays CPU, memory, pagefile, and system resource usage statistics. The Processes tab lists all active processes and a wide range of optional statistics. You can terminate any non-system process by highlighting it and then clicking End Process. You also can change the execution priority of an application from the Processes tab. Your options are Realtime, High, AboveNormal, Normal, BelowNormal, and Low. Avoid using Realtime so essential system operations are not disrupted. Only computer administrators can use Realtime.
- The Applications tab lists all active applications and their status. If an application is listed as Not responding, you can terminate it by highlighting it and then clicking End Task. However, be patient with seemingly nonresponsive applications. It is common for an application to perform some intense calculations and temporarily stop responding, only to return to normal operation after a few minutes.
- On the Visual Effects tab of the Performance Options dialog box (System applet, Advanced tab, Performance area Settings button) you can define what level of display effects are used. Selections can be made individually or you can select to let Windows choose what is best for my computer (default), best appearance, or best performance. To improve desktop responsiveness, select Adjust for best performance.

OBJECTIVES ON THE JOB

Desktop performance is a function of the CPU, memory, and disk subsystem interactions with the operating systems and software executing on that hardware. Using a powerful computer, efficient software, and intelligent configuration settings will improve the performance of the Windows XP desktop.

PRACTICE TEST QUESTIONS

1. The primary tool through which you can observe the performance of Windows XP is:
    a. Performance Monitor
    b. Network Monitor
    c. System Monitor
    d. System Information

2. Windows XP has 32 levels of execution priority. However, through the Processes tab of Task Manager, a user can assign a process only one of six priorities.
    a. True
    b. False

3. Through Task Manager, a user can terminate what type of applications and processes? (Choose all that apply.)
    a. Those not responding
    b. Those functioning normally
    c. Those started by the user
    d. Those started by the system

4. It is a good practice to immediately terminate any application if it stops responding to keyboard and mouse commands.
    a. True
    b. False

5. You should set the Visual Effects option to best appearance to improve desktop responsiveness.
    a. True
    b. False

6. If improperly tuned, the performance efficiency of the desktop can be adversely affected by which of the following subsystems? (Choose all that apply.)
    a. CPU
    b. Memory
    c. Network interface
    d. Hard drive

7. Use the Realtime execution priority with caution because it can cause a system failure.
    a. True
    b. False

OBJECTIVES

4.1.1 Optimize and troubleshoot memory performance

MEMORY OPTIMIZATION

UNDERSTANDING THE OBJECTIVE

Monitoring memory performance involves both the memory object and the disk objects. Memory is composed of RAM and the paging file.

WHAT YOU REALLY NEED TO KNOW

- Memory\Page Faults/sec: Number of page faults (hard [pulled from hard drive] and soft [pulled from RAM]) per second. An increasing value or a consistent value over 50 can indicate significant paging. This can be an issue if hard faults are prominent.
- Memory\Page Reads/sec: Number of disk reads (not pages) caused by hard page faults per second. An increasing value can indicate too much reliance on the paging file.
- Memory\Page Writes/sec: Number of disk writes (not pages) caused by paging. An increasing value can indicate too much reliance on the paging file.
- Memory\Pages Input/sec: Number of pages read from disk initiated by a hard page fault per second. An increasing value can indicate too much reliance on the paging file.
- Memory\Pages Output/sec: Number of pages written to disk per second. An increasing value can indicate too much reliance on the paging file.
- Memory\Available Bytes: Amount of free or available RAM. A value below 4 MB indicates a severe RAM shortage.
- Memory\Pool Nonpaged Bytes: The size of the nonpaged pool (those memory pages never saved to the paging file). Significant changes (10% or more) over the normal value may indicate problems with software or the operating system.
- To optimize memory, perform one or more of the following:
    - Install more physical RAM.
    - Replace existing RAM with faster RAM (60 ns is faster than 70 ns).
    - Upgrade to a faster hard drive and drive controller to improve paging file access.
    - Increase the maximum size of the paging file.
    - Split the paging file across multiple drives. Place the paging file on a different drive than the boot drive (that is, where the main Windows XP files reside).
    - Uninstall unnecessary applications, services, and protocols.
    - Add more cache to the motherboard.

OBJECTIVES ON THE JOB

All Microsoft operating systems and software benefit from additional fast RAM. When possible, fully populate the motherboard with RAM. When a paging file is used, be sure that it is on the fastest drive in the computer.

PRACTICE TEST QUESTIONS

1. When a system has too little RAM, what other subsystem will be most affected?
   a. CPU
   b. Network interface
   c. Hard drive
   d. Video and display

2. Which of the following counters may indicate a problem when its value slowly but steadily increases over time? (Choose all that apply.)
   a. Memory\Page Faults/sec
   b. Memory\Page Reads/sec
   c. Memory\Available Bytes
   d. Memory\Pool Nonpaged Bytes

3. A system needs more RAM when the Memory\Available Bytes counter falls below what value?
   a. 4 MB
   b. 8 MB
   c. 16 MB
   d. 32 MB

4. A value over 50 for Memory\Page Faults/sec can indicate a shortage in RAM when which of the following is true?
   a. The value of Memory\Pool Nonpaged Bytes remains constant.
   b. Fast User Switching is enabled.
   c. The CPU is over 60% utilization.
   d. Most page faults are hard page faults.

5. Memory optimization can be accomplished by performing what action? (Choose all that apply.)
   a. Replace 60 ns memory with 70 ns memory.
   b. Double the amount of RAM in a system.
   c. Remove unnecessary services from a system.
   d. Place the paging file on the same drive as the main Windows files.

6. A fast drive controller can help reduce the negative effect of virtual memory paging on the performance of a system.
   a. True
   b. False

7. In most cases, what is the best way to improve performance on any Microsoft operating system?
   a. Add more drive space.
   b. Use only bus-mastering adapters.
   c. Add more RAM.
   d. Reduce the cache on the motherboard.

OBJECTIVES

4.1.2 Optimize and troubleshoot processor utilization

PROCESSOR OPTIMIZATION

UNDERSTANDING THE OBJECTIVE

The CPU is rarely the primary bottleneck in a system. However, when it is underperforming, you should replace or upgrade it, or add additional CPUs.

WHAT YOU REALLY NEED TO KNOW

- Processor\% Processor Time: Indicates the percentage of time the CPU is performing work. A consistent value above 90% might indicate the CPU is overworked. If you have a multiprocessor system, look at Processor\% Total Processor Time.
- System\Processor Queue Length: Indicates the number of execution threads in the CPU's queue. Each CPU in a multiprocessor system has its own queue; the System\Processor Queue Length is the cumulative total of all CPU queues. A consistent value of two more than the number of processors indicates the CPU(s) are overworked.
- Process\% Processor Time: Indicates the percentage of time a specific process is using the CPU. If a single process consistently consumes most of the CPU activity, the process might be poorly written, be experiencing a problem, or the CPU is overworked.
- Process\% Privileged Time: Indicates the percentage of time that privileged (that is, kernel mode) processes have consumed the CPU. A sustained value over 90% may indicate the CPU is not powerful enough to support ongoing system upkeep in addition to user activities.
- Process\% User Time: Indicates the percentage of time that user-mode processes have used the CPU.
- To optimize the processor, perform one or more of the following:
    - Add an additional CPU or replace the current CPU with a faster one.
    - Change execution priorities for user-mode processes.
    - Add more L2, on-board, or secondary cache.
    - Disable all 3-D graphical screen savers.
    - Reduce the number of CPU-intensive applications on the system.
    - Replace the motherboard with one that has a faster bus speed.

OBJECTIVES ON THE JOB

As operating system technology moves forward, it is important to provide systems with as much computing power as possible. The CPU, while not usually the most glaring cause of system slowdown, is still an important element in providing sufficient computing power. Always install the fastest CPU available, and when feasible, use multiple CPUs.

PRACTICE TEST QUESTIONS

1. A consistent value over 90 for Processor\% Processor Time always indicates that the CPU is the bottleneck in a system.
   a. True
   b. False

2. A system is being asked to perform more work than it can adequately manage when the System\Processor Queue Length counter has what measurement?
   a. Two or more
   b. Two more than the number of CPUs
   c. Four
   d. One-quarter the number of MB of RAM in the system

3. If a single process consistently consumes most of the CPU activity, as measured by Process\% Processor Time, the process might be poorly written, be experiencing a problem, or the CPU is overworked.
   a. True
   b. False

4. A sustained value over 90% for which counter may indicate the CPU is not powerful enough to support ongoing system upkeep in addition to user activities.
   a. System\Processor Queue Length
   b. Process\% User Time
   c. Process\% Privileged Time
   d. Processor\% Processor Time

5. Which of the following most effectively lessens the load on a CPU?
   a. Remove unnecessary applications.
   b. Remove 3-D screen savers.
   c. Disable Fast User Switching.
   d. Disable Standby Mode.

6. Which of the following helps improve the performance of a system's processors? (Choose all that apply.)
   a. Replace the CPU with a faster model.
   b. Add a second CPU to the system.
   c. Use bus-mastering adapter cards.
   d. Add more L2, on-board, or secondary cache.

7. What part of a system, when upgraded, usually improves overall system performance?
   a. RAM
   b. CPU
   c. Network interface
   d. Video adapter

OBJECTIVES

4.1.3 Optimize and troubleshoot disk performance

DISK OPTIMIZATION

UNDERSTANDING THE OBJECTIVE

The drive subsystem is the second-most-common bottleneck cause (behind memory). When memory is insufficient, any deficiency of the drive subsystem becomes obvious. The responsiveness of a system depends on the efficiency of its hard drives.

WHAT YOU REALLY NEED TO KNOW

- ◆ PhysicalDisk\% Disk Time: Indicates the percentage of time a drive is busy performing read or write operations. A consistent value over 90% may indicate too much activity on the system for the drive subsystem or too much paging due to insufficient RAM.
- ◆ PhysicalDisk\Avg. Disk Queue Length or Current Disk Queue Length: The number of read and write requests queued for a drive. A consistent value of two more than the number of spindles in the drive indicates too much activity or a slow hard drive/controller.
- ◆ PhysicalDisk\Avg. Disk sec/Read and Avg. Disk sec/Write: Indicates the amount of time required to perform a drive operation. A consistent high value or an increasing value over time indicates a slow drive system.
- ◆ PhysicalDisk\Avg. Disk Bytes/Read and Avg. Disk Bytes/Write: Indicates the average rate of data transfer for a drive. A consistent value of 4 KB indicates that most drive activity is caused by paging. Additional RAM is required.
- ◆ To optimize the drive system, perform one or more of the following:
  - Install faster hard drives and drive controllers.
  - Separate CD-ROM and DVD drives from hard drives on drive controller chains.
  - Use **PCI** 32-bit bus-mastering drive controllers.
  - If using SCSI, be sure it supports asynchronous I/O to allow parallel operation of all drives on the chain.
  - Use hardware-based **RAID**. Avoid software RAID; it consumes CPU time and reduces overall performance.
  - Regularly defragment drives, scan for errors, perform drive cleanup, and delete unnecessary personal files.
  - Keep drive capacity below 50% when possible.
  - Avoid compression and encryption when performance is important.

OBJECTIVES ON THE JOB

A computer's hard drives always affect the system's speed. If RAM is insufficient, paging activities will be slowed by a poor drive subsystem. When adequate RAM is installed, the hard drives must be fast to provide a fast and efficient user experience.

PRACTICE TEST QUESTIONS

1. A consistent value over 90 for the _____ counter may indicate too much activity on the system for the drive subsystem or too much paging due to insufficient RAM.
    a. PhysicalDisk\Avg. Disk Queue Length
    b. PhysicalDisk\% Disk Time
    c. PhysicalDisk\% Disk sec/Read
    d. PhysicalDisk\Avg. Disk Bytes/Read

2. A consistent value of two more than the number of spindles in the drive for the PhysicalDisk\Avg. Disk Queue Length counter indicates too much activity or a slow hard drive/controller.
    a. True
    b. False

3. A consistent value of 4 KB for the _____ counter indicates that most drive activity is caused by paging and additional RAM is required.
    a. PhysicalDisk\Avg. Disk Queue Length
    b. PhysicalDisk\% Disk Time
    c. PhysicalDisk\% Disk sec/Read
    d. PhysicalDisk\Avg. Disk Bytes/Read

4. Which of the following causes the greatest load reduction on the drive subsystem?
    a. Disabling unnecessary services
    b. Storing only large files on the drives
    c. Adding RAM
    d. Keeping drive capacity under 50%

5. Which of the following drive optimization methods causes the least amount of strain on the system as a whole?
    a. A large paging file instead of installing more RAM
    b. Hardware RAID
    c. Software RAID
    d. ISA drive controllers

6. Separating CD-ROM and DVD drives from hard drives on drive controller chains improves hard drive performance.
    a. True
    b. False

7. From a hard drive perspective, which of the following should be avoided when speed is important? (Choose all that apply.)
    a. Compression
    b. Large drive sizes
    c. FAT
    d. Encryption

OBJECTIVES

4.1.4 Optimize and troubleshoot application performance

APPLICATION OPTIMIZATION

UNDERSTANDING THE OBJECTIVE

Improving application performance in Windows XP is related to the efficiency and speed of the hardware itself. However, some software controls can help improve application performance.

WHAT YOU REALLY NEED TO KNOW

- Install only necessary services and applications. The more software installed on a system, the more memory-resident components consume vital system resources.
- Increasing an application's execution priority can improve its performance. However, setting the priority too high can interfere with system sustainment activity by the kernel. Assign AboveNormal and High priorities, but avoid Realtime whenever possible.
- When using multiple Windows 16-bit applications, start each in a separate memory space to force them into separate virtual machines. Each **VM** will be executed in preemptive multiprocessing mode rather than in cooperative mode (as is the case within a Win16 VM with multiple 16-bit applications).
- DOS VMs are automatically removed after the application they supported is terminated.
- After a Win16 application is terminated, Windows XP retains the Win16 VM. If other Win16 applications are not used immediately, terminating the empty VM improves system performance. WOWEXEC operates within a DOS VM (NTVDM process). On the Processes tab of Task Manager, use the End Process button to terminate the WOWEXEC process. Terminating WOWEXEC causes Windows XP to terminate the supporting NTVDM process.
- Regularly check the Event Viewer's Application log for details on information, warnings, and errors related to applications. A failing or underperforming application may be improved through knowledge gained from the log.
- Windows XP can customize DOS VM environments by using CONFIG.NT and AUTOEXEC.NET, which replace the CONFIG.SYS and AUTOEXEC.BAT files found on DOS-only systems. Windows XP can provide a wide range of memory customizations, including extended, expanded, **DPMI**, and HIMEM.SYS.
- On the Advanced tab of the Performance Options dialog box (System applet, Advanced tab, Performance area Settings button) you can set processor scheduling and memory allocation to focus on programs or background services. A client system should have both set for programs (the default).

OBJECTIVES ON THE JOB

If an application consistently performs unsatisfactorily, it might be poorly coded. Replace the application with a more efficient product. To improve overall application performance, use the most powerful computer system possible, add additional RAM, or improve the drive subsystem.

PRACTICE TEST QUESTIONS

1. Which of the following are good practices to improve application performance?
    a. Install only necessary services.
    b. Install all possible protocols, but bind them in use-priority order.
    c. Set execution priority to BelowNormal.
    d. Use only Windows 16-bit applications.

2. Increasing an application's execution priority can improve its performance, but setting it too high can cause system failures.
    a. True
    b. False

3. When multiple Windows 16-bit applications are started, they are executed within a single virtual machine by default.
    a. True
    b. False

4. After a DOS program is completed, the VM created by the NTVDM process remains active and must be manually terminated.
    a. True
    b. False

5. The name of the process that emulates the Windows 16-bit environment is:
    a. NTVDM
    b. Win16
    c. Win31
    d. WOWEXEC

6. The environment into which a DOS application is executed can be customized using what files?
    a. AUTOEXEC.BAT
    b. CONFIG.NT
    c. WIN.INI
    d. SYSTEM.INI

7. In most cases, application performance can be improved by which of the following?
    a. Reviewing Event Viewer
    b. Using visual effects
    c. Adding RAM
    d. Disabling network access

OBJECTIVES

4.1.5 Configure, manage, and troubleshoot Scheduled Tasks

SCHEDULED TASKS

UNDERSTANDING THE OBJECTIVE

The Scheduled Tasks utility is used to automate the execution of programs and batch files.

WHAT YOU REALLY NEED TO KNOW

- You can schedule a task to be run at a specific time, repeated at intervals, started at system startup, started at user logon, or started when the system is idle.
- Tasks can be executed under any user's security context if the user name and password are provided when the task is defined.
- The Add Scheduled Task Wizard creates a basic task definition, but a complete set of options can be accessed only through a task's properties.
- Defined tasks can be moved from one system to another. You can also edit and manage tasks on remote systems—Windows 95, Windows 98, Windows NT, Windows 2000, and Windows XP—assuming the remote system has remote Registry access enabled and the administrative share for the drive hosting the task definitions is still active.
- Scheduled tasks can be created by other applications, such as the Backup tool. You can also use the command-line AT utility to schedule tasks.
- Troubleshooting a scheduled task involves verifying that all settings are correct, double-checking the time, AM/PM, and repeat interval, and double-checking that the path to the application or batch file is correct. You should also verify that any parameters used for an application or the scripting within a batch file are correct.
- If a task fails to execute, check that the Enabled check box on the Task tab of the task's Properties dialog box is marked.
- The status of tasks is displayed in the Scheduled Tasks window. There are four possible values: Blank—task is not running or has run and completed successfully; Running—the task is currently running; Missed—one or more of the scheduled executions for this task were missed; and Could not start—the last attempt to start this task failed.
- The SchedLgU.txt file records the activity of scheduled tasks. This file may offer insight as to why a task failed or why a task stopped during its execution.

OBJECTIVES ON THE JOB

The ability to schedule tasks greatly simplifies an administrator's workload. By taking a few extra moments to create a scheduled task, many management actions, such as backup and antivirus scanning, can be set once and forgotten.

PRACTICE TEST QUESTIONS

1. Windows XP offers the ability to schedule tasks to start: (Choose all that apply.)
    a. at a specific time
    b. at system startup
    c. at logoff
    d. after an idle period

2. Tasks can be scheduled to execute only under the security context of a computer administrator.
    a. True
    b. False

3. From the Windows XP Scheduled Tasks utility, you can remotely manage tasks on what other system? (Choose all that apply.)
    a. Windows 98
    b. Windows NT
    c. Windows 2000
    d. Windows 3.1

4. Which of the following is a possible reason that a task fails to execute? (Choose all that apply.)
    a. The security context is defined as a system administrator.
    b. AM was selected when PM was needed.
    c. The Enabled check box on the Tasks tab was not marked.
    d. An incorrect path to the batch file was defined.

5. Which of the following status values could indicate that the application defined in the task is no longer present on the system?
    a. Blank
    b. Running
    c. Missed
    d. Could not start

6. The Scheduled Tasks log file might provide information as to why a task was terminated prematurely.
    a. True
    b. False

7. Tasks defined on one system cannot be moved to another without completely reconfiguring the task definition.
    a. True
    b. False

OBJECTIVES

4.2 Manage, monitor, and optimize system performance for mobile users

MOBILE USER OPTIMIZATION

UNDERSTANDING THE OBJECTIVE

Windows XP includes numerous features focused on maximizing productivity for mobile users. These features include Offline Files, hardware profiles, and power management. To get the most out of Windows XP on portable systems, make sure the hardware is ACPI-compliant.

WHAT YOU REALLY NEED TO KNOW

- Define a hardware profile for each configuration or hardware situation. For example, define a Network profile for connecting to the office **LAN**, which has the modem disabled, and a Dialup profile for dialing into the Internet, which has the NIC disabled.
- When both an NIC and a modem are present and enabled on a system, bind the NIC in priority order to the modem.
- Use Offline Files to maintain access to files when disconnected from the network. Set this feature to synchronize files at logoff and to not synchronize over slow links.
- Standby saves the system state to RAM, which will be lost if battery power is exhausted. Hibernation saves to the hard drive and can withstand battery failure.
- If using encryption, always export the encryption key to removable media, delete the key from the local system, and define another user account (preferably not the default computer administrator) as the key recovery agent.
- If using folder redirection, configure Offline Files to store redirected folders so that the files in them are accessible when not connected to the network.
- When operating on battery power, configure the system to hibernate and turn off the monitor and hard disks after a certain number of idle minutes. This extends battery life.
- You can configure scheduled tasks to execute when working from battery power or to stop if battery mode begins.
- Use the Battery Status object in System Monitor to measure and view the charge rate, discharge rate, remaining capacity, and the voltage of the battery.
- The user of a portable system should be a member of the local Power Users group. Then the user can install and remove software and drivers while away from the office, network, and system administrator.

OBJECTIVES ON THE JOB

Configuring and optimizing Windows XP on a portable system is based more on common sense than on unique operating strategies.

PRACTICE TEST QUESTIONS

1. To take advantage of the myriad features designed to optimize Windows XP on a portable system, that system must support:
    a. high-speed network connections
    b. IrDA
    c. ACPI
    d. a docking station

2. The office network has a strict policy that no modem connections can be made from network clients. However, your laptop computer has a built-in modem. How can you comply with office requirements and still use the modem when traveling?
    a. Have the vendor remove the modem and then use a PC Card modem only when away from the office.
    b. Create two local user accounts, grant one access to the modem and restrict the other, and only use the restricted account when connected to the network.
    c. Create hardware profiles for network connectivity and traveling.
    d. Use group policies to disable the modem.

3. When optimizing offline files for a portable system, which of the following is an important setting? (Choose all that apply.)
    a. Synchronize on system logon and logoff
    b. Restrict cached files to 10 MB
    c. Don't synchronize over slow links
    d. Cache accessed files only

4. _____ saves the state of the system to memory where it can be quickly restored. However, if the battery power fails, the system state data is lost.
    a. Hibernation
    b. Shutdown
    c. Fast User Switching
    d. Standby

5. Deleting the SAM database file from a Windows XP system deletes all user accounts and resets the Administrator password to blank. Which of the following actions prevents a thief from using this tactic to regain access to encrypted materials on the hard drive? (Choose all that apply.)
    a. Define the recovery agent as the Administrator.
    b. Define the recovery agent as any user but the Administrator.
    c. Export the recovery key to removable media and delete it from the system.
    d. Encrypt the entire hard drive.

6. To simplify administration on the road, portable system users should be members of the local Power Users group.
    a. True
    b. False

OBJECTIVES

4.3 Restore and back up the operating system, system state data, and user data

BACK UP • RESTORE

UNDERSTANDING THE OBJECTIVE

Protecting the operating system, system state data, and user data usually involves a two-step process. First, you must perform preventive measures, often in the form of a backup. Second, you must perform repair and restore measures to return the system to a stored state.

WHAT YOU REALLY NEED TO KNOW

- System state data is protected in two ways in Windows XP: via the Last Known Good Configuration or a backup.
- The **LKGC** is an advanced startup option. You access it by pressing F8 when the startup menu is displayed on multiboot systems, or just before the graphical Windows XP splash screen is displayed on a single operating system. This tool starts Windows XP using the state of the Registry recorded at the moment of the last successful logon. This is often a good first-step recovery technique after installing a bad driver or encountering a system that doesn't start normally.
- Protecting the system state data through a backup means the data is stored on backup media and must be restored using the Backup utility. The native Backup tool and almost all compatible backup products can save and restore the memory-resident system state data. Restoring such system state data returns the system to the configuration at the time of the backup.
- The \repair subdirectory in the main Windows directory contains the compressed Registry files that Windows XP stores across restarts. Manually backing up this folder provides you with a resource location to restore all or part of the Registry (system state data) using one of the Registry editing tools (Regedit, Regedt32, or Regrest) or the Recovery Console.

OBJECTIVES ON THE JOB

The most dependable way to protect system state data, the operating system, or even user data is to create a reliable backup of that data before any problems occur. Without a backup, any remaining recovery attempt options don't offer much of a solution. You should use a backup product that performs automated backups of all systems on the network.

PRACTICE TEST QUESTIONS

1. You downloaded a new driver for your sound card. Using the Update button on the Driver tab of the device's Properties dialog box, you install the new driver. You are prompted to restart. However, just before the logon box is displayed, the system crashes. What should be your first step to return the system to a working state?
   a. Use the Recovery Console.
   b. Roll back the driver.
   c. Use the LKGC.
   d. Use the Repair process.
   e. Restore the old driver from a backup.

2. You log on to your Windows XP system and promptly install new drivers for your video card. After you restart the system, the screen image is distorted but still legible, so you log on. You attempt to change the video settings to improve the display. You restart, but now you cannot read the screen image. You restart again and choose the Last Known Good Configuration. What will be the status of the screen image?
   a. Exactly as it was before the new video drivers were installed
   b. Completely distorted
   c. Distorted but legible
   d. The system will not boot.

3. Using the scenario from Question 2, after choosing Last Known Good Configuration, what should you do to restore the system to normal?
   a. Nothing, the system is returned to pre-driver installation normal by starting with the Last Known Good Configuration.
   b. Use the Recovery Console to restore the system state data from backup.
   c. Click the Roll Back Driver button to remove the new video driver.
   d. Reinstall Windows XP.
   e. Use the Last Known Good Configuration to restart a second time.

4. How can you use the Last Known Good Configuration to restore a system?
   a. Select it from the Shutdown options.
   b. Press F8 during startup before the GUI splash screen appears.
   c. Hold down the Ctrl key during startup.
   d. Through the Repair process started from the bootable distribution CD.

5. System state data must be backed up as a separate process from operating system or user data files.
   a. True
   b. False

6. If you have a backup of the \repair folder on removable media, it can be used to replace a damaged Registry section through the Recovery Console.
   a. True
   b. False

OBJECTIVES

4.3.1 Recover system state data and user data by using Windows Backup

WINDOWS BACKUP

UNDERSTANDING THE OBJECTIVE

Windows XP includes a native Backup utility. This utility can be used to back up any file on the local system and on remote networked systems. This utility offers a specific selection of system state data so memory-resident information will be saved to the backup media.

WHAT YOU REALLY NEED TO KNOW

- You can back up and restore local and remote files using the Windows XP Backup utility. Remote files can be accessed through user-defined shares or the default administrative shares created by the operating system (c$, d$, and so on).
- The Backup utility backs up system state data from the local machine only. This option is not available for remote systems.
- You can schedule backup jobs to occur at a specific time, daily, weekly, monthly, at system startup, at user logon, or when the system is idle. A scheduled backup can be terminated after it runs for a specified length of time or prevented if battery mode starts.
- You cannot schedule restore operations. Restored files can be returned to their original location, an alternate location while maintaining their directory structure, or all files can be deposited into a single directory (discarding the saved directory structure). When restoring, you can elect to not replace any existing file, replace an existing file if it's older than the backed-up version, or always replace files.
- Backups can be initiated manually through the GUI utility, through the wizard, or from the ntbackup command line tool. The command line tool can also be used in batch files. Restores can be initiated manually through the GUI utility or through the wizard.
- Backup offers five types of backups:
  - Normal: All selected files are copied to the backup media; the archive bit is reset.
  - Copy: All selected files are copied to the backup media; the archive bit is not reset.
  - Daily: All selected files that have been modified the same day the backup is executed are copied to the backup media; the archive bit is not reset.
  - Incremental: All selected files that have been changed since the last normal or incremental backup (that is, since the archive bit was set) are copied to the backup media; the archive bit is reset.
  - Differential: All selected files that have been changed since the last normal or incremental backup (that is, since the archive bit was set) are copied to the backup media; the archive bit is not reset.

OBJECTIVES ON THE JOB

The native Windows XP Backup utility is useful for stand-alone systems, but is not adequate for true network protection. It is very important to automate your backup procedure and swap your media to provide a safety net for your data, operating system, and system state.

PRACTICE TEST QUESTIONS

1. Match the following statements (1–6) with one or more of the five backup types (a–e). Assume the backup set is all possible files on the local hard drive.
    1. Creates a copy of every selected file every time it is used.
    2. Resets the archive bit.
    3. Captures all files changed within the last 25 hours (assuming no other backup has occurred in that time period).
    4. Copies all changed files, and only changed files, since the last backup.
    5. The best option for work-in-progress backups to a removable media.
    6. When used following a normal backup on a daily basis, provides a means to restore an entire system using only two backup media sets (the normal set and the set created using this backup type).
       a. Normal
       b. Copy
       c. Daily
       d. Incremental
       e. Differential

2. Which backup type clears the archive bit? (Choose all that apply.)
    a. Normal
    b. Copy
    c. Daily
    d. Incremental
    e. Differential

3. Which backup set offers the fastest restoration path for a system that must be completely restored from backup?
    a. Daily incremental
    b. Weekly copies and regular daily backups
    c. A normal with daily incrementals
    d. A normal with daily differentials

4. You've configured the backup schedule on your Windows XP system as follows (the backups always initiate at 11:00 p.m.):

   Friday–normal backup

   Monday, Wednesday, Saturday–incremental backup

   Tuesday, Thursday, Sunday–differential backup

   A thunderstorm on Thursday morning damages the hard drive. You rebuild the operating system and need to restore your user data files and other critical files as quickly as possible. What is the best strategy?
    a. Restore the backups made on Friday, then Thursday.
    b. Restore the backups made on Friday, then Wednesday.
    c. Restore the backups made on Friday, then Tuesday, then Wednesday.
    d. Restore the backups made on Friday, then Monday, then Tuesday, then Wednesday.

OBJECTIVES

4.3.2 Troubleshoot system restoration by starting in safe mode

SAFE MODE

UNDERSTANDING THE OBJECTIVE

Advanced startup options in Windows XP can often aid in restoring a system and circumventing bad drivers, software, and configurations.

WHAT YOU REALLY NEED TO KNOW

- ◆ You access the Advanced options menu by pressing F8 when the startup menu is displayed for multiboot systems, or by pressing F8 when the Starting Windows text message appears just before the GUI Windows XP splash screen appears.
  The boot menu options include:
  - Safe Mode: Starts with minimal drivers and system files—VGA, mouse, keyboard, storage, and essential services, no network support.
  - Safe Mode with Networking: Starts in Safe Mode with non-PC card network support.
  - Safe Mode with Command Prompt: Starts in Safe Mode with Command Prompt, not with GUI.
  - Enable Boot logging: Turns on recording of data about loaded drivers to NTBTLOG.TXT.
  - Enable VGA Mode: Turns on minimal VGA support for non-Safe Mode boots— 800 x 600 with 256 or 16 colors.
  - Last Known Good Configuration (LKGC): Uses the Registry status saved at the moment of the last successful logon.
  - Directory Services Restore Mode (domain controllers only): Rebuilds Active Directory.
  - Debugging Mode: Transmits debugging and boot progress data over the serial port to be captured by a second system (see the Windows XP Resource Kit).
- ◆ If the system will not start and display the logon prompt, even after attempting LKGC, try Safe Mode. While in Safe Mode, attempt to uninstall drivers or software that were added, or reverse configuration settings that may have caused the problem.
- ◆ Safe Mode with Networking works only on systems that don't use PC Card network interfaces, because PC Card support drivers are not loaded in Safe Mode. Use this startup method when network access is required to perform a system repair or when files/drivers/software is only available on a network share.
- ◆ Safe Mode with Command Prompt offers you the power of the Windows XP environment without the GUI desktop interface. Using command line tools, you can accomplish most repair tasks. To return to normal operation, you must restart.

OBJECTIVES ON THE JOB

Safe Mode offers an additional method to restore a system. Safe Mode and a reliable backup solution are typically all the recovery tools a system administrator will need.

PRACTICE TEST QUESTIONS

1. You installed drivers for a new video card. After restarting, the screen image is distorted and not legible. You press Ctrl+Alt+Del, type your password, and then press Enter. You somewhat recognize your desktop, but the screen image is still too distorted to read anything or determine the location of icons and the mouse pointer. Which of the following should you try to restore the system's video? (Choose all that apply.)
   a. Restart using the Roll Back Driver button on the Driver tab of the video card's Properties dialog box.
   b. Restart using Safe Mode.
   c. Restart using Safe Mode with Command Prompt.
   d. Restart using Directory Services Restore Mode.

2. Using a different computer, you visit the video card vendor's Web site. You discover that the drivers shipped with the product were damaged during duplication. You download new functioning drivers and copy them to a floppy. The instructions state that the best method to install the drivers is to manually replace the files already on the system. What is the best mode to boot into to perform this operation?
   a. Directory Services Restore Mode
   b. Safe Mode with Command Prompt
   c. Debugging Mode
   d. No mode will enable this process.

3. Which of the following issues may be resolved using Safe Mode? (Choose all that apply.)
   a. Missing protocol driver
   b. A corrupted service
   c. Unable to communicate with domain controller
   d. Sound card driver corrupted
   e. Network component driver preventing system startup
   f. Corrupted Registry

4. Safe Mode with Command Prompt could be used to restore a system if a core video driver fails, preventing display of the GUI interface of Windows XP.
   a. True
   b. False

5. Safe Mode can be used only by an administrator.
   a. True
   b. False

6. In most cases, Safe Mode with Networking allows a laptop computer to access network shares of software required to repair the system.
   a. True
   b. False

OBJECTIVES

4.3.3 Recover system state data and user data by using the Recovery Console

RECOVERY CONSOLE

UNDERSTANDING THE OBJECTIVE

The Recovery Console is a command line interface to Windows XP, and can be used to perform numerous restoration actions to try to return a system to working order. Through Recovery Console, all local drives can be accessed, the Registry can be manipulated, and services can be configured.

WHAT YOU REALLY NEED TO KNOW

- The Recovery Console is not installed by default. Installing the Recovery Console so it can be accessed through the startup menu requires the execution of winnt32 /cmdcons from the Windows XP distribution CD. Starting the Recovery Console from the setup process requires booting the computer with the Setup boot disks or the distribution CD, choosing R (for repair), and then choosing C (for Recovery Console) when prompted.
- The Recovery Console is operated by using command line utilities. These utilities can be used to perform a wide range of operations, including to replace files (such as drivers, services, or Registry storage files), configure services, format hard drives, configure drivers, repair boot sectors, and perform several common file and folder operations (such as move, copy, rename, and delete).
- You must be a member of the Administrators group to use the Recovery Console.
- To view a complete list of commands and syntax that can be used within the Recovery Console, issue the help command from within the Recovery Console, view the Recovery Console section of the Windows XP Help and Support Center, or consult the Windows XP Resource Kit.
- When in the Recovery Console, corrupted, damaged, or deleted files can be replaced from backups stored on local hard drives or from local removable media (floppies or CDs). You can also disable or enable services and drivers that may be hampering the normal operation of the system. If you have a backup of the Registry files available, you can replace them in the \repair directory.
- By default, the Recovery Console is configured to prevent writing files to floppies or other removable media. You change this by enabling the Recovery Console: Allow floppy copy and access to all Files and all Folders security option in the **LCP**. You can also enable automatic administrative logon for the Recovery Console through the LCP.

OBJECTIVES ON THE JOB

The Recovery Console is an advanced troubleshooting tool. It does not offer quick fixes or easy solutions as do Safe Mode boot options. Instead, unless you are familiar with the interworkings of your system, know which component is failing, and have replacement files, the Recovery Console does not offer much help in a crisis. Plan ahead and become familiar with your system, and the Recovery Console value increases when you run out of other options.

PRACTICE TEST QUESTIONS

1. **The Recovery Console may offer a resolution option in which of the following situations? (Choose all that apply.)**
    a. A boot failure occurs due to a new video driver.
    b. A hard drive is no longer accessible through its drive letter.
    c. The sam._ Registry file has been deleted.
    d. A user account has been deleted.
    e. The boot sector of the primary hard drive is corrupt.
    f. A system resource conflict exists between the NIC and a new sound card.
    g. The system is unable to function due to a newly installed service, which is consuming the CPU's processing cycles.

2. **How can the Recovery Console be started? (Choose all that apply.)**
    a. Start RecCon from the Run dialog box.
    b. Install the Recovery Console using the winnt32 /cmdcons command, and then use the startup menu.
    c. Through the Shutdown command
    d. Boot from the distribution CD, and then select the appropriate choices.

3. **The Recovery Console can be used to: (Choose all that apply.)**
    a. create new user accounts
    b. access all hard drives on the local system
    c. replace the Registry files stored in the \repair folder
    d. copy files to a floppy by default
    e. disable a newly installed service
    f. remove a software application
    g. alter the settings of a Scheduled Task
    h. reformat a hard drive

4. **Any user account can be used to access the Recovery Console.**
    a. True
    b. False

5. **You can alter the LCP to allow which of the following in relation to the Recovery Console?**
    a. Auto logon of all user accounts
    b. Disable access to NTFS-formatted volumes
    c. Enable file copy to removable media
    d. Enable network access

6. **When Windows XP is installed, the Recovery Console is also installed by default.**
    a. True
    b. False

7. **From within the Recovery Console, you can access all of the tools found in the Administrative Tools section of the Control Panel.**
    a. True
    b. False

Section 5

Configuring and Troubleshooting the Desktop Environment

OBJECTIVES

5.1 Configure and manage user profiles

USER PROFILES

UNDERSTANDING THE OBJECTIVE

User profiles are the desktop settings, Start menu items, and general environmental configurations that can follow a user from one system to another on a network.

WHAT YOU REALLY NEED TO KNOW

- By default, each user who logs on to Windows XP receives a unique user profile. Initially this profile is a duplicate of the default user profile. Also, by default, all user profiles save any changes to that profile at user logoff.
- A mandatory profile allows a user to change his or her environment while logged on, but all changes are discarded and not saved to the profile when the user logs off. The next time the user logs on, the original profile is displayed. You create mandatory profiles by renaming the NTUSER.DAT file to NTUSER.MAN. Two or more users can share a mandatory profile.
- User profiles are local by default only. To create roaming profiles, define a network share path for the storage of the profile in the user account's properties on a domain controller. Roaming profiles are available on domains only, not workgroups.
- You delete, copy, and change a profile's type (roaming or local) in the User Profiles dialog box (accessed by clicking the Settings button under User Profiles on the Advanced tab of the System applet). A roaming profile can be converted to a local profile using this tool, but a local profile cannot be converted to a remote profile.
- The Guest account has a profile, but it does not retain changes upon user logoff.
- Profiles are stored in the \Documents and Settings folder under the name of the user account. A copy of a user's roaming profile is stored locally on each machine the user logs on to.
- To change or alter a user profile, you must log on as the user/owner of that profile and make changes directly to the environment and desktop. This does not apply to mandatory profiles.

OBJECTIVES ON THE JOB

The disadvantage of roaming profiles is that the larger the profile, the longer it takes to log on and log off. Group policies can be configured to prevent some portions of a profile such as Temporary Internet Files, History, Local Settings, and Temp from being uploaded to the network share. Outlook stores the main .pst file and the default archive file within the Local Settings hierarchy.

PRACTICE TEST QUESTIONS

1. A mandatory profile can be shared by multiple users without causing conflicts.
    a. True
    b. False

2. When a user logs on to a Windows XP system for the first time (assuming the user does not already have a roaming profile defined), a new profile is created by duplicating what other preexisting profile?
    a. Administrator
    b. Last logged on user
    c. All users
    d. Default user

3. A roaming profile can be used both on domains and workgroup networks.
    a. True
    b. False

4. A roaming profile is stored on a network share and on each system the user logs on to.
    a. True
    b. False

5. In what situation will the changes made to a user's environment not be recorded to a profile when the user logs off? (Choose all that apply.)
    a. When the user is the administrator
    b. When the user is a guest
    c. When the user is a domain member
    d. When the user has a mandatory profile

6. Once a profile becomes a mandatory profile, it is not possible to make further permanent changes.
    a. True
    b. False

7. Which of the following creates a roaming profile for an existing user account?
    a. Change the profile path statement for the user account on the local system.
    b. Change the profile path statement for the user account on the domain controller.
    c. Change the type setting in the User Profiles dialog box to remote.
    d. Rename the NTUSER.DAT file to NTUSER.MAN.

OBJECTIVES

5.2 Configure support for multiple languages or multiple locations; enable multiple-language support; configure multiple-language support for users; configure local settings; configure Windows XP Professional for multiple locations

MULTIPLE LANGUAGES

UNDERSTANDING THE OBJECTIVE

Windows XP is designed to elegantly support multiple languages. Switching between languages is as easy as a few mouse clicks or a hot key sequence.

WHAT YOU REALLY NEED TO KNOW

- ◆ You configure languages through the Regional and Language Options applet. The default standard formatting for numbers, currencies, dates, and time is defined on the Regional Options tab. A drop-down list offers a plethora of predefined country/language/region-specific selections, or you can fully customize the formatting.
- ◆ You can also use the Regional Options tab to define the location or local setting. This setting defines your primary country of residence and is used by online services (such as **MSN**) to provide relevant information such as news and weather.
- ◆ On the Languages tab, you can elect to install files for complex script and right-to-left languages (including Thai) and/or install files for East Asian languages. Click the Details button to select the language services installed on the system. To make multiple languages available, add them in this dialog box.
- ◆ Use the Language Bar to quickly switch between installed languages with a mouse click. You can also define hot keys to switch between languages.
- ◆ On the Advanced tab, use non-Unicode programs to define the language used in menus and dialog boxes. This setting applies to all users of this computer and does not affect Unicode programs.
- ◆ All installed languages are accessible by all users. The settings for default languages and standards apply only to the current user, with two exceptions. The first is the Unicode setting. The second is selecting the Apply all settings to the current user account and to the default user profile option on the Advanced tab. Choosing this option makes your settings the default for all new user profiles created on this system.
- ◆ Windows XP can be defined to use only a single location at a time through the Regional and Languages Options applet. However, through the Phone and Modem Options applet, you can define multiple locations used for defining dial-out parameters. A dialing location includes various details such as country/region, area codes, accessing an outside line, carrier codes, disabling call waiting, and long-distance calls.

OBJECTIVES ON THE JOB

Most U.S. keyboards support only a limited range of characters. Use a specialized keyboard for languages with significantly more characters than English.

PRACTICE TEST QUESTIONS

1. To install Japanese as a second language on your Windows XP system, what must you do? (Choose all that apply.)
    a. Select Japanese as a Unicode format.
    b. Add the Japanese service as an input language.
    c. Mark the Install files for East Asian languages check box.
    d. Customize the Standards and Formats setting.

2. **The Language Bar is used to:**
    a. install additional languages
    b. quick-switch between installed languages
    c. convert text from one language to another
    d. perform word and page counts

3. **An installed language is accessible only to the user who installed the language service.**
    a. True
    b. False

4. **Multiple users use the same client system. One user prefers to work with English as their primary input language, while the other users prefer Arabic and German. Which of the following is true?**
    a. All users of a single system use the same default input language.
    b. Each user of a single system can have a unique setting for their default input language.
    c. Each user should install the language service needed by their preferred input language and uninstall all others.
    d. The Language Bar should be disabled so users cannot switch between input languages.

5. **You travel extensively around the globe. In each country, you perform financial audits and produce detailed reports. You are required to format these reports using the standards and formats common to each region. Which of the following actions is the most sensible to accomplish this?**
    a. Change the default input language as you enter each country.
    b. Define a unique location through Phone and Modem Options for each country or region.
    c. Customize the standards and formats options for each country or region as you enter that area.
    d. Change the setting on the Regional Options tab of the Regional and Language Options applet as you enter each country or region.

6. **You use the location setting in the Regional and Language Options applet to:**
    a. define the input language
    b. set the standards and formats for the system
    c. aid online services in providing relevant information such as news and weather based on your location
    d. select the hardware profile

OBJECTIVES

5.3 Manage applications by using Windows Installer packages

WINDOWS INSTALLER

UNDERSTANDING THE OBJECTIVE

Windows Installer simplifies the task of deploying, patching, repairing, and removing software on systems. Through a single set of setup rules, an entire network's software base can be managed.

WHAT YOU REALLY NEED TO KNOW

- ◆ The Windows Installer tool is the msiexec executable, which can be used to install and configure software (with the /i parameter), repair software (/f), uninstall software (/x), and apply patches (/p), among others.
- ◆ Windows Installer can apply or install three types of packages on a system: .msi (software installation), .msp (patches, service packs, and software updates), and .mst files (transformation or modification files, used to customize an installation).
- ◆ These packages are often found on the distribution CD of major software, such as Microsoft Office. You can create your own installer packages using any number of third-party tools, such as VERITAS WinINSTALL LE, InstallShield, Wise Solutions, or Microsoft Visual Studio Installer.
- ◆ When using msiexec to repair a software product, you can elect to reinstall missing files, reinstall files if the current file is a different version, reinstall all files, and repair user-specific Registry entries, among others.
- ◆ Through Group Policy, you can control how Windows Installer works. Controls include disable Windows Installer, always install with elevated privileges, disable rollback, disable patching, enable user control over installs, allow admin to install from Terminal Services session, disallow user installs, disable creation of System Restore checkpoint, and enable logging.

OBJECTIVES ON THE JOB

Through Windows Installer and Group Policy, you can force software installations, patches, repairs, and even removal of software from client systems. You can also offer optional software products to users, which, if desired, they can choose to install. (This is known as advertising a package.) The msiexec tool itself cannot be used to create an installer package; it is used to deploy packages.

PRACTICE TEST QUESTIONS

1. **The Windows Installer tool can be used to: (Choose all that apply.)**
   a. install applications
   b. update software
   c. alter client system configuration, such as desktop settings
   d. repair software
   e. create installer packages

2. **Windows Installer can use an installer package with which extension? (Choose all that apply.)**
   a. .msi
   b. .msc
   c. .mst
   d. .msp

3. **You must use a third-party tool to create Windows Installer packages for any software you wish to deploy.**
   a. True
   b. False

4. **A repair action using Windows Installer can elect to: (Choose all that apply.)**
   a. replace all files
   b. replace only files older than those in the installer package
   c. replace only missing files
   d. replace all files with a different version than those in the installer package

5. **Windows Installer can be configured so that it does not create a System Restore Checkpoint when installing a new software package.**
   a. True
   b. False

6. **It is not possible for an administrator to install a Windows Installer package through a Windows Terminal Services session.**
   a. True
   b. False

7. **The Windows Installer can be disabled through Group Policy.**
   a. True
   b. False

OBJECTIVES

5.4 Configure and troubleshoot desktop settings

DESKTOP SETTINGS TROUBLESHOOTING

UNDERSTANDING THE OBJECTIVE

Desktop settings can include a wide range of configuration options such as video display settings, sound schemes, visual effects, the Start menu, desktop icons, and screen savers. Anything that affects how the desktop operates or appears can be considered a desktop setting. Troubleshooting desktop settings requires understanding how each setting is made, what can go wrong, and how to make corrections.

WHAT YOU REALLY NEED TO KNOW

- Altering the display properties or replacing the video driver can result in an unreadable display. To return the system to working order, restart using the LKGC. However, if that fails, restart again in VGA mode. From there you can usually access the Display applet to set options that are compatible with your components. For options available on the Settings tab of the Display applet, see Objective 3.2.
- If you delete or move an item from the Start menu or the desktop, you can usually get it back by pressing Ctrl+Z (undo last command). If that fails, check the Recycle Bin for the deleted item. In most cases it can be restored. However, the Recycle Bin only captures files deleted by My Computer and Windows Explorer interfaces, not those files deleted by other applications.
- The Start menu can be edited directly using right-click commands, with drag and drop actions, or through a My Computer or Windows Explorer interface (right-click over the Start menu and select Open or Explore).
- Use the Display applet to select or define a theme, select background images, set desktop color, select and change desktop icons, add Web components to the desktop, select and configure the screen saver, select a display style and color scheme, configure effects, and customize window and button colors and fonts. In most cases, troubleshooting a setting mistake simply requires that you reopen the applet and change the setting to something more appropriate for your system.

OBJECTIVES ON THE JOB

Configuring desktop settings and troubleshooting problems is most often accomplished by using common sense and backtracking your steps. The Control Panel houses nearly every control used to manipulate the desktop, so you should thoroughly familiarize yourself with all controls.

PRACTICE TEST QUESTIONS

1. **If you install a video driver that fails, what should you do first to repair your system?**
    a. Roll back the driver.
    b. Use the Recovery Console.
    c. Reboot using the LKGC.
    d. Reinstall Windows XP.

2. **Regarding Question 1, if your first course of action fails, what is the next best action to take?**
    a. Reinstall Windows XP.
    b. Boot using VGA mode.
    c. Use the Recovery Console.
    d. Switch hardware profiles.

3. **If you regret making a change to a file, icon, or item in the Start menu, and that was the last action you've taken, what is the first thing you should do to reverse the change?**
    a. Empty the Recycle Bin.
    b. Reboot the system.
    c. Use System Restore and restore the last checkpoint.
    d. Press Ctrl+Z.

4. **The Start menu can be customized using which of the following actions? (Choose all that apply.)**
    a. Right-click over a Start menu item.
    b. Open the System applet.
    c. Use drag and drop.
    d. Edit the folder structure through Windows Explorer.

5. **In most cases, troubleshooting a desktop setting mistake simply requires that you reopen the applet and change the setting to something more appropriate for your system.**
    a. True
    b. False

6. **Every deleted file is captured by the Recycle Bin.**
    a. True
    b. False

7. **When working in the Display applet, you can reverse most setting mistakes by reopening the applet and making a different option selection. However, changes made through or on the Settings tab of this applet can require a reboot using the LKGC or VGA mode.**
    a. True
    b. False

OBJECTIVES

5.5 Configure and troubleshoot accessibility services

ACCESSIBILITY SERVICES

UNDERSTANDING THE OBJECTIVE

Windows XP is more accessible to special needs users than previous Windows operating systems. Windows XP includes numerous features and configuration settings that make interaction with the operating system easier for users with mobility, vision, or hearing impairments.

WHAT YOU REALLY NEED TO KNOW

- Accessibility services are primarily configured through the Accessibility Options applet.
- Keyboard controls include StickyKeys, FilterKeys, and ToggleKeys. StickyKeys enables use of the Ctrl, Shift, or Alt keys by pressing once; holding is not required. FilterKeys ignores quick or repeated keystrokes. ToggleKeys plays a tone when the Caps Lock, Scroll Lock, or Num Lock key is depressed.
- Sound controls include SoundSentry and ShowSounds. SoundSentry displays visual clues such as a title bar, window, or the desktop when the system plays a sound. ShowSounds displays captions when sounds or speech are played.
- Display controls include High Contrast and cursor options. High Contrast sets the Windows display to a high-contrast color scheme to facilitate reading. Cursor options allow you to change the blink rate and width of the cursor.
- Mouse controls include MouseKeys, which allows you to control the mouse using the numeric keypad. You can also use several general controls. With general controls you can turn off accessibility features after a number of idle minutes, display warning messages when turning on a feature, play a sound when a feature is turned on or off, use SerialKeys to support alternate input devices, and apply all settings to the logon desktop. You can also choose whether to apply all settings as the default for new users.
- Windows XP also includes Magnifier, Narrator, On-Screen Keyboard, Utility Manager, and an Accessibility Wizard. Magnifier uses the top one-sixth of the display to show a magnified view (two to nine times) of the area around the mouse cursor. Narrator can be configured to read the contents of displayed documents and dialog boxes. On-Screen Keyboard can be used to enter text using a mouse, a pointing device, or a SerialKey input device. The Utility Manager is used to control whether Magnifier, Narrator, and On-Screen Keyboard utilities are automatically run at logon. The Accessibility Wizard is a step-by-step guide to configuring Windows XP for maximum usability for mobility-, vision-, or hearing-impaired users.
- Troubleshooting accessibility services involves double-checking the settings selected for each service offered and enabling or disabling services as needed.

OBJECTIVES ON THE JOB

Some accessibility options are useful even if you are not impaired. For example, MouseKeys can be used anytime you either don't have a mouse or don't have space to use one.

PRACTICE TEST QUESTIONS

1. Windows XP is designed to be accessible to as many potential users as possible, including those who are mobility, vision, or hearing impaired.
    a. True
    b. False

2. Match the following accessibility services with their description:
    1. StickyKeys
    2. FilterKeys
    3. ToggleKeys
    4. SoundSentry
    5. ShowSounds
        a. Plays a tone when Caps Lock, Scroll Lock, or Num Lock is depressed
        b. Enables use of the Ctrl, Shift, or Alt keys by pressing once; holding is not required
        c. Displays captions when sounds or speech are played
        d. Ignores quick or repeated keystrokes
        e. Displays visual clues such as a title bar, window, or the desktop when the system plays a sound

3. Cursor options allow you to set the cursor shape.
    a. True
    b. False

4. MouseKeys allows you to control the mouse using a customizable set of keys from any part of the keyboard.
    a. True
    b. False

5. Windows XP supports alternate input devices for those users who are unable to use a standard keyboard or mouse.
    a. True
    b. False

6. Magnifier can display a zoomed-in view of the screen around the mouse cursor at a magnification level of two to _____ times.
    a. four
    b. six
    c. nine
    d. 12

7. Troubleshooting accessibility services involves double-checking the settings selected for each service offered and enabling or disabling services as needed.
    a. True
    b. False

Section 6

Implementing, Managing, and Troubleshooting Network Protocols and Services

OBJECTIVES

6.1 Configure and troubleshoot the TCP/IP protocol

TCP/IP

UNDERSTANDING THE OBJECTIVE

TCP/IP is the preferred network protocol on Microsoft networks. TCP/IP is required to communicate over the Internet. When dialing into an **ISP**, your TCP/IP configuration is usually defined automatically. On a network, your Windows XP system might require manual IP configuration.

WHAT YOU REALLY NEED TO KNOW

- For a Windows XP system to participate on a network, it needs an IP address and a subnet mask. These can be obtained automatically from DHCP (by default). To communicate outside its own local subnet, a gateway is required.
- More advanced settings include DNS servers, **WINS** servers, multiple IP addresses, using LMHOSTS, enabling/disabling **NetBIOS** over TCP/IP, and TCP/IP filtering.
- You define TCP/IP settings through the Properties dialog box of each network connection object. Each network connection object has independent TCP/IP configurations.
- When TCP/IP communications fail, first verify that your settings are correct. Then, use the ipconfig /all command to verify that the intended settings are in effect. Be sure that the settings match the correct adapter, that IP addresses are not repeated, and the correct subnet mask and gateway are used.
- If your settings are correct but communication still fails, check physical connections (including the NIC connection to the network media), update the NIC driver, and restart the system.
- If your settings are correct, physical connections are secure, and the NIC driver is updated, ping another system within your subnet. Next, ping the gateway address, then the gateway address in another subnet, and then another system in another subnet. If you're connected to the Internet, ping any system on the Internet. The general location of the communication failure is determined when one of these tests fail.
- Test to see if other clients in the same subnet reproduce the communication failure.
- If IP address connections work but domain name or NetBIOS name connections fail, investigate the name resolution services.

OBJECTIVES ON THE JOB

TCP/IP configuration on clients is usually very simple and straightforward. In most larger networks, DHCP is used. Smaller networks often use manually assigned addresses and not the high-end, complex TCP/IP services. Larger networks that use the high-end services typically use DHCP to autoconfigure clients.

PRACTICE TEST QUESTIONS

1. Windows XP always requires manual configuration of TCP/IP when connected to a network.
    a. True
    b. False

2. Which of the following items is strictly required to communicate over the Internet through a dial-out connection? (Choose all that apply.)
    a. IP address
    b. Subnet mask
    c. Default gateway
    d. WINS server address

3. Windows XP can be configured not use to NetBIOS over TCP/IP.
    a. True
    b. False

4. If TCP/IP configuration settings are correct but communication still fails, what other course of action should you take? (Choose all that apply.)
    a. Reinstall Windows XP.
    b. Install NWLink.
    c. Update the device driver for the NIC.
    d. Restart the system.

5. To view the TCP/IP configuration settings for every network connection on a system, what command should you use?
    a. ping /route
    b. telnet -127.0.01
    c. ipconfig /all
    d. nbtstat -R

6. If you can connect to a remote system when you provide the IP address, but the connection fails when you provide the domain name for the same system, what is the most likely problem?
    a. A physical disconnect exists between your system and the remote system.
    b. The default gateway is improperly configured.
    c. The name resolution system is failing.
    d. NetBIOS has been disabled.

7. The PING utility can help determine the approximate location of a communication interruption by testing systems close to the current client and then progressively testing systems further away.
    a. True
    b. False

OBJECTIVES

6.2 Connect to computers by using dial-up networking; connect to computers by using a virtual private network (VPN) connection; create a dial-up connection to connect to a remote access server; connect to the Internet by using dial-up networking; and configure and troubleshoot Internet Connection Sharing

DIAL-UP NETWORKING

UNDERSTANDING THE OBJECTIVE

Windows XP supports numerous types of network connections, including typical LAN links, and dial-up, **VPN**, and Internet connections. Network links are managed through Network Connections.

WHAT YOU REALLY NEED TO KNOW

- Dial-up networking can be used to establish a network link between a Windows XP system and an ISP, a network, or a stand-alone system.
- You can establish a VPN connection between Windows XP and a remote system or network through an Internet link. The VPN link uses **PPTP** or **L2TP** to provide secured communications, uses the IP address of the answering system, and encrypts logon credentials and all transferred data. The VPN protocol is predetermined or set to Auto.
- To create a remote connection you must have a phone number, and you must select the type of server (**PPP** or **SLIP**) and configure network components, such as TCP/IP and Client for Microsoft Networks. Windows XP supports PPP on incoming connections. A PPP connection can include TCP/IP, NWLink, or VPN protocols.
- To create a connection to the Internet you must have a phone number, and you must set the server type to PPP and configure TCP/IP for DHCP.
- Any dial-up connection object can be shared with other clients through Internet Connection Sharing. **ICS** is designed for use on small networks, and should not be used on networks with DNS servers. Also, because ICS provides basic DHCP services for its clients, no other DHCP servers should be present on the network.
- When ICS is enabled, the system becomes a demand-dial router. The local NIC is assigned 192.168.0.1 and 255.255.255.0. Other clients must be configured for DHCP to use the shared connection. Clients are assigned an IP configuration in the 192.168.0.0 network.
- Use the Settings button on the Sharing tab to define services Internet users can access over the ICS link. Predefined services include **FTP**, L2TP, PPTP, **IMAP3**, IMAP4, **SMTP**, **IKE**, **POP3**, Remote Desktop, Web (**HTTP** and **HTTPS**), and Telnet. Other services can be added by properly defining their respective TCP and **UDP** ports.
- To troubleshoot ICS, check local network connectivity, terminate and re-create the shared dial-up link, verify dial-up connection settings, and reset clients to use DHCP.

OBJECTIVES ON THE JOB

ICS is an inexpensive mechanism to share a single network connection. However, as your network grows, ICS cannot adequately manage your connectivity needs. As Internet traffic increases, the performance of the ICS host system will degrade.

PRACTICE TEST QUESTIONS

1. A VPN link between a Windows XP client and a Windows 2000 Server system will always offer encrypted authentication and data transfer through L2TP.
    a. True
    b. False

2. Other than a network connection between the two systems, what item is needed to establish a VPN link?
    a. Administrative access
    b. IP address of host system
    c. NWLink
    d. NAT proxy

3. Windows XP can accept which type of incoming connection? (Choose all that apply.)
    a. PPP
    b. SLIP
    c. VPN
    d. NWLink

4. Dial-up connections to ISPs, especially for home users, are typically configured to use a:
    a. manually-configured IP address
    b. software-controlled VPN link
    c. third-party-enhanced Web browser
    d. DHCP-assigned IP address

5. For Internet Connection Sharing to be used on a network, which of the following must be true? (Choose all that apply.)
    a. A DHCP server is present.
    b. A DHCP server is not present.
    c. A DNS server is present.
    d. A DNS server is not present.
    e. Clients are configured for DHCP.
    f. Clients are manually configured to use any IP address.
    g. It must be enabled on a dial-up connection.

6. By default, ICS allows which of the following services to be accessed by internal clients using the ICS link to gain Internet access? (Choose all that apply.)
    a. Web
    b. FTP
    c. IRC
    d. E-mail
    e. VPNs
    f. All Internet services

OBJECTIVES

6.3 Connect to resources using Internet Explorer

INTERNET EXPLORER

UNDERSTANDING THE OBJECTIVE

Windows XP includes Internet Explorer 6.0. **IE** can be used to access many types of resources, including Web, FTP, and local.

WHAT YOU REALLY NEED TO KNOW

- Internet Explorer can be used to connect to Internet Web resources. Web resources can be unsecured (HTTP) or secured (HTTPS). To access a site, you must enter its URL in either the Address text box or through File, Open. The URL can include the prefix "http://" or "https://", but it is not necessary.

- Internet Explorer can be used to connect to FTP resources. To access a site, you must enter its URL in either the Address text box or through File, Open. The URL can include the prefix "ftp://", but once the browser attempts communication with the site, it recognizes it as an FTP server and not a Web server, so typing the prefix is not necessary. If the FTP site is open for public anonymous access, IE will log you on anonymously. If the FTP site requires user authentication, a dialog box prompting for user name and password appears. A URL can be constructed that includes the user name and password: ftp://*username:password*@ftp.*site.name*/. FTP logon credentials are always transmitted in clear text.

- You can access local resources through the File, Open command, or by dragging and dropping the resource on IE. URLs displayed in other applications, such as Outlook Express, usually start an IE window to display the resource when the URL is clicked.

- Locating resources is easy using the built-in IE Search tool. You can use a normal language question or query to locate information, products, files, or Web sites.

- Using Favorites, you can bookmark sites you wish to revisit. Favorites can be reaccessed either through the Favorites menu in Internet Explorer, or in Windows Explorer, My Computer, or the Start menu.

- Use the Media button to access the integrated Windows Media Player content site to explore multimedia presentations on entertainment, technology, news, and more.

- Using History, you can return to a Web site you visited in the past but didn't mark as a Favorite. The History list can be searched by keyword and is sorted by the current day, day of the week, last week, and weeks ago.

- Use the Back and Forward buttons to navigate single pages in reverse or forward with a single click, or jump up to 10 pages in either direction through the drop-down arrow.

OBJECTIVES ON THE JOB

Internet Explorer is the primary tool used by Windows XP to access non-e-mail Internet resources. IE 6 offers an easy-to-use, intuitive interface for interacting with Web content.

PRACTICE TEST QUESTIONS

1. Internet Explorer can be used only to view Web content.
    a. True
    b. False

2. Internet Explorer requires that you type the prefix for every resource when entering a URL.
    a. True
    b. False

3. Internet Explorer can be configured to transmit encrypted FTP logon credentials.
    a. True
    b. False

4. Which of the following is a valid construction syntax form for accessing a secured FTP site? (Choose all that apply.)
    a. *ftp.mysite.com*
    b. *ftp://ftp.mysite.com/*
    c. *ftp://johng:PushMonkey5@ftp.mysite.com/*
    d. *ftps://ftp.mysite.com/*

5. Online resources marked in Favorites can be accessed through which tool? (Choose all that apply.)
    a. System applet
    b. Internet Explorer
    c. Windows Explorer
    d. Start menu

6. You can search the History list using keywords.
    a. True
    b. False

7. Internet Explorer allows quick-jump navigation of 10 pages back with only a few mouse clicks.
    a. True
    b. False

OBJECTIVES

6.4 Configure, manage, and implement Internet Information Services (IIS)

INTERNET INFORMATION SERVICES

UNDERSTANDING THE OBJECTIVE

IIS is included with Windows XP. IIS can be used to host Web and FTP sites for a maximum of 10 simultaneous users because of license restrictions.

WHAT YOU REALLY NEED TO KNOW

- IIS is not installed by default. Once installed, it can be managed through the IIS applet in Administrative Tools.
- Resources offered through IIS Web and FTP sites should be access controlled on an NTFS file level, rather than relying on the IIS internal controls alone.
- The default roots for IIS are \InetPub\wwwroot and \InetPub\ftproot off the boot partition. However, IIS sites can use any local or network folder as their root.
- Placing files with appropriate access permissions in the site roots makes those files available to visitors.
- IIS sites can be anonymous only, authorized user only, or mixed. Web authorization can be configured securely, but FTP authentication is always in clear text.
- The IUSR_<systemname> account is used to authenticate anonymous users.
- A single IIS system can host multiple Web sites off multiple IP addresses or the same IP address. For systems with only a single IP address, different Web sites are distinguished using host headers. Host headers are defined through the Advanced button located alongside the IP Address text box on the Web Site tab of the Properties dialog box of a Web site. Each unique Web site should be assigned its own host header. A host header is usually a word, short phrase, domain name, or title that the Web site administrator uses as the distinguishing element for that site. The Web user never sees the host header. If host headers are not used, a Web user would always see the first or default Web site hosted by the one-IP-address IIS Web server, even if they used the URL or domain name of any other Web site hosted by that Web server.

OBJECTIVES ON THE JOB

IIS on Windows XP is a great tool for sharing files and hosting small intranet Web sites. However, Windows XP is not an appropriate platform to host a public Internet Web site because of its license restrictions on simultaneous users and its preconfigured system tuning for user applications.

PRACTICE TEST QUESTIONS

1. Internet Information Services is installed by default on Windows XP.
    a. True
    b. False

2. The Windows XP IIS can provide what type of service? (Choose all that apply.)
    a. Web
    b. E-mail
    c. FTP
    d. Telnet

3. Access controls to resources accessed through IIS Web sites should be primarily controlled by:
    a. subnet structure
    b. NTFS file-level access permissions
    c. site-level controls
    d. bandwidth throttles

4. IIS's default root directories must be used for all Web sites.
    a. True
    b. False

5. IIS can be configured to require encrypted transmission of FTP logon credentials.
    a. True
    b. False

6. A Windows XP system with IIS is used to host three Web sites: *bobsshed.com*, *sueskitchen.com*, and *billysbeef.com*. However, regardless of the URL entered, end users are always served the *bobsshed.com* Web site. Why?
    a. The wrong subnet mask is defined on the Windows XP IIS system.
    b. The clients are not using TCP/IP.
    c. The DNS system is damaged.
    d. The Windows XP system is using only a single IP address.

7. The exact host header for a Web site must be entered by the end user when attempting to access a secondary Web site on a Windows XP IIS system that has only a single IP address.
    a. True
    b. False

OBJECTIVES

6.5 Configure, manage, and troubleshoot remote desktop and remote assistance

REMOTE DESKTOP • REMOTE ASSISTANCE

UNDERSTANDING THE OBJECTIVE

Remote Desktop enables a remote user to log on to a system and perform activities as if they were physically at that system. Remote Assistance is used to invite another user to view and/or interact with your desktop while you are logged on.

WHAT YOU REALLY NEED TO KNOW

- Remote Assistance supports remote viewing of the current desktop, real-time interaction with the current desktop, file exchange, and real-time chat (voice and text).
- The end user initiates a Remote Assistance session by sending an invitation to a support staff member. The invitation can be sent through Windows Messenger or standard e-mail as an attachment. Remote Assistance invitations have an expiration time limit and can have a password defined to prevent unauthorized use.
- When using Remote Assistance, both the remote and local systems must run Windows XP or newer with either Windows Messenger Service or a MAPI-compliant e-mail utility (such as Outlook Express), and must have network or Internet connectivity. The faster the connectivity between the two systems, the more responsive the control.
- Remote Desktop is used to connect to a system from a remote location. Instead of creating a typical network link, it creates a terminal-host link in which your remote display, keyboard, and mouse act as if they are physically connected to the system you've logged into. Within a Remote Desktop session, you can interact with the system as if you were physically present.
- Remote Desktop is made possible either by using the IIS Remote Desktop Web Connection or through the Remote Desktop Connection utility. The IIS tool allows the connection to be initiated through Internet Explorer. The Remote Desktop Connection tool can be used in Windows XP, Windows 2000, or Windows 98 to connect to a Windows XP system. This tool is found on the Windows XP distribution CD. Both remote tools are enabled on the Remote tab of the System applet.
- If Remote Assistance fails, you can troubleshoot it by checking the expiration date of the invitation, reissue the invitation with a revised expiration date and password, check network connectivity between the two systems, make sure Remote Assistance is enabled, and make sure both systems are Windows XP.
- If Remote Desktop fails, you can troubleshoot it by checking network connectivity between the two systems, make sure Remote Desktop is enabled, and check that the user account has been granted access.

OBJECTIVES ON THE JOB

Remote Assistance is useful when training new employees or just lending a hand to a co-worker. Remote Desktop is useful when traveling users need access to their desktop workstations.

PRACTICE TEST QUESTIONS

1. Which remote tool requires the use of an invitation?
    a. Remote Assistance
    b. Remote Desktop

2. The remote tools require or can require authentication?
    a. True
    b. False

3. Which remote tool can be used in Windows XP, Windows 2000, or Windows 98 to connect to a Windows XP system?
    a. Remote Assistance
    b. Remote Desktop Connection

4. Which remote tool typically requires a person at each end of the connection for the tool to be useful?
    a. Remote Assistance
    b. Remote Desktop

5. If an invited support staff member cannot establish a Remote Assistance connection, which of the following troubleshooting actions should you attempt? (Choose all that apply.)
    a. Check the invitation's expiration date.
    b. Verify the invitation password.
    c. Reinstall Windows XP.
    d. Check network connectivity.

6. If you cannot make a Remote Desktop connection from your home system to the office computer, which of the following troubleshooting actions should you attempt? (Choose all that apply.)
    a. Check network connectivity.
    b. Verify that ICS is enabled.
    c. Verify user account access permission.
    d. Verify that Remote Desktop is enabled on the office computer.

7. Which remote tool requires the presence of Windows Messenger Service or a MAPI-compliant e-mail utility?
    a. Remote Assistance
    b. Remote Desktop

OBJECTIVES

6.6 Configure, manage, and troubleshoot an Internet connection firewall

INTERNET CONNECTION FIREWALL

UNDERSTANDING THE OBJECTIVE

Internet Connection Firewall is a security control that is designed to restrict unauthorized and unrequested traffic from passing from outside sources into a network or system.

WHAT YOU REALLY NEED TO KNOW

- ◆ **ICF** can be enabled on any network interface on Windows XP. Microsoft recommends using ICF on every connection object that links with a system outside your total control, except for VPN links. ICF is not available on incoming connection objects.
- ◆ ICF is a stateful firewall. Stateful firewalls inspect every packet that passes through the protected interface. Generally, ICF prevents all traffic that was not specifically requested from entering the system.
- ◆ ICF can be configured to allow specific types of traffic to enter without a corresponding request. Typically, these traffic types are services that Internet or external users request from your system. They are defined on the Services tab of the Advanced Settings for ICF. Microsoft predefined the services of FTP, IMAP3, IMAP4, SMTP, POP3, Remote Desktop, HTTPS, Telnet Server, and HTTP. Other services can be defined through their TCP and UDP ports.
- ◆ A log of the traffic handled by ICF can be recorded. Logging options are to log dropped packets and/or log successful connections. The Pfirewall.log file is located in the main Windows folder by default. Logging is defined on the Security Logging tab of the Advanced Settings for ICF.
- ◆ The ICMP tab of the Advanced Settings for ICF defines how ICF will respond to **ICMP** (ping) requests. By default, no action is taken, and all ICMP packets are dropped. Options include allowing incoming echo, timestamp, mask, and router requests; allowing outgoing destination unreachable, source quench, parameter problem, and time exceeded messages; and allowing redirects.
- ◆ The log contents can expose problems on your system. For example, if you discover that many inbound port 80 packets are being accepted, you have a Web server operating on your system. If this is not intentional, you have a security problem.
- ◆ When problems occur that may involve ICF, test network connectivity with ICF both enabled and disabled, recheck ICF settings, or restart the system.

OBJECTIVES ON THE JOB

ICF is a welcome addition to the Windows product line. The proliferation of shared bandwidth Internet links, such as cable modems, has made personal firewalls a necessity. ICF offers all the security a typical home user needs, and offers an inexpensive solution for business users.

PRACTICE TEST QUESTIONS

1. Internet Connection Firewall is what type of firewall?
    a. Stateless
    b. Static
    c. Stateful
    d. Circuit

2. When initially enabled, the default of ICF is: (Choose all that apply.)
    a. allow all traffic in both directions
    b. allow all inbound traffic
    c. allow all outbound traffic
    d. allow inbound traffic that was requested

3. After installing Windows XP on a new computer and connecting it to your cable modem, you decide to enable ICF to protect your files from unwanted viewers. You enable logging and choose to log all activity. A few weeks later you look at the contents of the log file and discover several connections to port 80 on your system from an external system. What does this indicate?
    a. You've been surfing the Web.
    b. You've downloaded files from a Web site.
    c. A rogue Web server is active on your system.
    d. Someone is using Remote Desktop to control your system.

4. You've just installed IIS with all of its possible components as well as a third-party server to support IRC chats on your Windows XP system. You've enabled ICF to prevent unwanted traffic, but want to configure ICF to allow Internet users to access your Web, FTP, and IRC services. You don't have a clue about the TCP or UDP ports in use by these services. Which of these services can you allow ICF to pass to your system without tracking down additional configuration information?
    a. Web
    b. FTP
    c. IRC
    d. None of the above

5. When an external user pings your system, which is protected by ICF, what occurs? (Assume the default configuration of ICF.)
    a. No response.
    b. A response is generated stating this system is protected by ICF.
    c. A ping flood is returned.
    d. The ping's IP address and packet contents are recorded to the log file.

6. ICF can be used to protect what type of connection on Windows XP? (Choose all that apply.)
    a. Normal LAN
    b. Dial-up
    c. VPNs
    d. Direct connection guest
    e. Direct connection host

Section 7

Configuring, Managing, and Troubleshooting Security

OBJECTIVES

7.1 Configure, manage, and troubleshoot Encrypting File System (EFS)

EFS • RECOVERY AGENT

UNDERSTANDING THE OBJECTIVE

The **EFS** helps protect user data from unauthorized access. EFS can be used to encrypt NTFS files, folders, and entire drives. Only the person who encrypted a file object can access that file object.

WHAT YOU REALLY NEED TO KNOW

- Files are encrypted by marking the Encrypt contents to secure data check box in the Advanced Attributes dialog box of a file object's properties.
- Encryption is an attribute of a file object; therefore, it behaves in the same manner as any other attribute in copy and move actions.
- EFS uses a recovery agent to restore access to encrypted file objects if the original user's decryption key is lost or damaged. EFS must have a defined recovery agent to function. The local Administrator is defined as the recovery agent until you specify another user. The recovery agent is defined through the group policy within the Public Key Policies section.
- Generally, assigning a domain administrator or some other administrative-level user account as the recovery agent is preferable over using the local Administrator. If the **SAM** database file is deleted, the local Administrator password is reset to blank, thus allowing anyone access, even to EFS-protected files.
- The EFS decryption key should be exported to removable media and deleted from the hard drive. This prevents user-account compromise, which can result in a malicious person accessing EFS-protected data. Each time decryption is required, the system prompts you for the decryption key. This action is performed using the Secpol.msc **MMC** snap-in.
- The recovery agent decrypts files by deselecting the Encrypt contents to secure data check box on the Advanced Attributes dialog box of a file object's properties.
- The Cipher command-line tool can be used to encrypt or decrypt files and folders.
- EFS-protected files are encrypted only while stored on the hard drive; they are decrypted when used by an application or transferred over the network.
- Most EFS failures are due to lost decryption keys. Use the recovery agent to decrypt file objects.
- Encryption and compression are mutually exclusive.
- Do not delete user accounts that have used EFS to protect files, otherwise you must rely on the recovery agent to decrypt files.

OBJECTIVES ON THE JOB

EFS offers an additional layer of protection for portable systems. Even an NTFS-bypassing tool that invalidates access permission controls cannot access the contents of EFS-protected files. However, this protection is only good if the decryption key is not stored on the system.

PRACTICE TEST QUESTIONS

1. **The default EFS recovery agent is:**
   a. the local Administrator
   b. the Guest user
   c. the Domain user
   d. any member of the Power Users group

2. **The file Mybudget.doc is encrypted with EFS. It is the only encrypted file object on your system. You move it from drive C: to drive E:. The resultant file will be:**
   a. encrypted
   b. decrypted
   c. locked
   d. corrupted

3. **The only way for a portable computer to be protected by EFS is to: (Choose all that apply.)**
   a. encrypt the entire hard drive
   b. format all volumes with FAT32
   c. define any user account other than the local Administrator as the recovery agent
   d. copy the decipher key onto removable media and delete it from the system

4. **How does the recovery agent recover files encrypted by a lost decryption key?**
   a. Files are restored from backup.
   b. The recovery agent creates a new decryption key.
   c. The recovery agent re-encrypts the files with their key to clear the old key, then decrypts the files with the agent's key.
   d. The recovery agent just decrypts the files.

5. **The EFS key, after it has been used to encrypt files on a system, cannot be removed from that system.**
   a. True
   b. False

6. **Once a file is protected by EFS, it is encrypted at all times, even when used by an application or in transit over a network.**
   a. True
   b. False

7. **What command-line tool can be used to encrypt and decrypt file objects?**
   a. Cipher
   b. Encrypt
   c. Protect
   d. Efslock

OBJECTIVES

7.2 Configure, manage, and troubleshoot local security policy

LOCAL SECURITY POLICY

UNDERSTANDING THE OBJECTIVE

The local security policy defines a range of controls that affect the security of the local system.

WHAT YOU REALLY NEED TO KNOW

- If your system is a stand-alone, the local security policy is the only policy that applies to this system. However, if you are a member of a domain, there can be numerous other policies that apply to this system. In every case, the local security policy has the least application priority, so its settings are often overwritten or superceded by a domain-based policy.
- When multiple policies are applicable, they are applied in the following order: Windows NT 4.0 NTCONFIG.POL file, local group policy, site group policies, domain group policies, then any **OU** group policies. Each subsequent policy overwrites the previous policy.
- The cumulative result of all applicable policies is the effective policy.
- The local security policy contains several subpolicies, including: account policies (password policy and account lockout policy, see Objective 7.3.2); local policies (audit policy, see Objective 7.3.1); user rights assignments (security options, see Objective 7.3.3); public key policies (EFS, see Objective 7.1); software restriction policies; and IP security policies.
- You can configure over 60 security options. These include disabling the Guest account, renaming the Administrator account, allowing format and eject of removable media, allowing server operators to schedule tasks, preventing the display of last user name, manipulating smart card removal behavior, disconnecting users when logon hours expire, and clearing virtual memory pagefile.
- Software-restriction policies control the ability of software to operate on the local system. This is primarily used to prevent unreliable code from being executed.
- IP security policies define how the system reacts to requests to establish secure communications with other systems.
- Troubleshooting local group policy involves double-checking all settings and restarting the computer to reapply the policy.

OBJECTIVES ON THE JOB

The local security policy should be defined on any system that is regularly disconnected from the network. Even though domain policies will still be in effect on disconnected systems because of caching, the local security policy provides security controls in the event that the cache fails.

PRACTICE TEST QUESTIONS

1. The local security policy is present only on Windows XP systems that are members of a domain.
    a. True
    b. False

2. When a Windows XP system is a member of a domain, the local security policy has the _____ application priority of all applicable policies.
    a. most
    b. least
    c. superficial
    d. average

3. When a Windows XP system is a member of a domain, what is the application priority of all possible policies?
    a. OU group policies, domain group policies, site group policies, local group policy, Windows NT 4.0 NTCONFIG.POL file
    b. Windows NT 4.0 NTCONFIG.POL file, local group policy, domain group policies, OU group policies, site group policies
    c. Windows NT 4.0 NTCONFIG.POL file, local group policy, site group policies, domain group policies, OU group policies
    d. Local group policy, Windows NT 4.0 NTCONFIG.POL file, site group policies, OU group policies, domain group policies

4. The cumulative result of all applicable policies is the _____ policy.
    a. standard
    b. default
    c. local
    d. effective

5. The local security policy contains several subpolicies, including: (Choose all that apply.)
    a. password policy
    b. runtime policy
    c. account lockout policy
    d. audit policy
    e. logon/logout policy
    f. administration policy
    g. user rights assignment
    h. security options
    I. remote access policy
    j. public key policies
    k. IP security policies

6. One security options setting allows format and eject of removable media.
    a. True
    b. False

OBJECTIVES

7.3 Configure, manage, and troubleshoot local user and group accounts; configure and troubleshoot local users and groups; configure, manage, and troubleshoot account settings

USERS • GROUPS • ACCOUNT SETTINGS

UNDERSTANDING THE OBJECTIVE

All access to Windows XP is controlled through user accounts and group memberships. Local user accounts and groups can be created and managed on the local system. Domain users and group memberships are managed on a domain controller.

WHAT YOU REALLY NEED TO KNOW

- Windows XP offers two types of user accounts: local accounts and domain accounts. Local accounts exist only on the local system. Local accounts are either created from scratch or by copying some aspects of an existing domain user account.
- Accounts are created or managed through two utilities: User Accounts applet in Control Panel or the Local Users and Groups tool accessed through User Accounts or Computer Management.
- When Windows XP is a member of a domain, the User Accounts applet can only be used to create domain user account duplicates, while the Local Users and Groups tool can be used to create user accounts from scratch.
- Local groups are created through the Local Users and Groups tool. Local groups can have local user accounts, domain user accounts, local groups, and domain groups as members.
- Microsoft recommends, when working within a domain, using local groups to assign access to resources, then making global groups members of the local groups and placing domain user accounts in the global groups.
- Default local groups in Windows XP as a domain member are: Administrators, Backup Operators, Guests, HelpServicesGroup, Network Configuration Operators, Power Users, Remote Desktop Users, Replicator, and Users.
- Account settings include access permissions, preferences (stored in profiles), and security settings, all of which are covered in detail in various sections of this book.
- If users experience trouble accessing resources, double-check their group memberships and the access permissions assigned to them.
- If users cannot log on, check that they are using the correct password and that they have logon rights to the system.

OBJECTIVES ON THE JOB

Only within a domain is user and group management a significant activity, but in that case it is managed from the domain controller and not the client system. On stand-alone systems, user and group management is present, but on a more modest scale.

PRACTICE TEST QUESTIONS

1. **What type of user account can be created on a Windows XP system as a member of a domain?**
   a. Domain user account
   b. Local user account
   c. Global user account
   d. Stand-alone user account

2. **How are local accounts created? (Choose all that apply.)**
   a. From scratch
   b. Using the Files and Settings Transfer Wizard
   c. Automatically by Windows XP
   d. By copying domain user accounts

3. **Local groups can have which of the following as a member? (Choose all that apply.)**
   a. Local user account
   b. Domain user account
   c. Local group
   d. Domain group

4. **The Microsoft recommendation for associating users with resources when working within a domain is represented by which of the following?**
   a. local group < domain users < resource < domain group
   b. resource < local group < domain group < domain users
   c. domain users < local group < domain group < resource
   d. domain group < resource < domain users < local group

5. **Network Configuration Operators is a default local group on a Windows XP system when it is a member of a domain.**
   a. True
   b. False

6. **If users complain that they cannot access a resource, which of the following is a valid troubleshooting technique? (Choose all that apply.)**
   a. Delete all local groups.
   b. Verify that all group memberships are valid.
   c. Change user accounts to be members of the Power Users group.
   d. Verify that the desired access permissions are properly defined.

7. **If a user cannot log on, what troubleshooting step(s) should you take? (Choose all that apply.)**
   a. Reinstall Windows XP.
   b. Verify the password.
   c. Check their local group memberships.
   d. Check their user rights.

OBJECTIVES

7.3.1 Configure, manage, and troubleshoot auditing

AUDITING

UNDERSTANDING THE OBJECTIVE

Auditing is the mechanism by which administrators can obtain a record of the activities that occurred on a system.

WHAT YOU REALLY NEED TO KNOW

- Auditing is enabled through the audit policy within the local security policy.
- There are nine audit policies: audit account logon events, audit account management, audit directory service access, audit logon events, audit object access, audit policy change, audit privilege user, audit process tracking, and audit system events.
- All policies are disabled by default. To enable them, you must set them to record events on a success and/or failure basis.
- All audited events are recorded in the Security Log accessed through Event Viewer. The audit event recorded in the Security Log includes all relevant details related to the audited occurrence.
- To record object access events, you must also configure auditing on each object you wish to track. Auditing is configured on objects by opening their Properties dialog box, clicking the Security tab, clicking Advanced, and then clicking the Auditing tab.
- Each object has a unique list of services or activities that can be audited. Each of these services or activities must be enabled on a success and/or failure basis on a user and/or group basis. For example, a folder object can audit listing a folder, reading attributes, creating new folders, and deleting folders.
- By default, auditing settings are inherited by all child objects. However, you can fully configure the inheritance of auditing by electing which child objects, if any, will have the inherited audit settings applied and whether this child object will accept audit configuration changes from parent objects.
- Troubleshooting auditing generally involves verifying the settings for success/failure for the audit policy, and then verifying the settings on each audited object.
- Too much auditing can result in system performance degradation, especially if all successful accesses to objects by authorized users are audited.

OBJECTIVES ON THE JOB

It is important to have a reason for auditing and know what you are looking for in the audit trail. Too much auditing can result in an overabundance of event details. Narrow your focus to a small set of activities or objects to make auditing easier to manage and auditing results easier to decipher.

PRACTICE TEST QUESTIONS

1. Auditing is enabled by default to track logons and logoffs in Windows XP.
   a. True
   b. False

2. Auditing is enabled through:
   a. System applet
   b. Windows Explorer
   c. local security policy
   d. Computer Management

3. To track the attempted compromise of a user account through repeated brute force password attempts, you should enable failure auditing on which policy?
   a. Audit system events
   b. Audit logon events
   c. Audit process tracking
   d. Audit object access

4. If you suspect a user has stolen membership in the Administrators group and is modifying configurations of user accounts, which of the following audit policies should you set to audit for Success? (Choose all that apply.)
   a. Audit account logon events
   b. Audit system events
   c. Audit account management
   d. Audit privilege user

5. What audit policy requires additional configuration before any audit events will be recorded?
   a. Audit system events
   b. Audit logon events
   c. Audit process tracking
   d. Audit object access

6. By default, the audit settings on a folder object will be inherited by all child objects.
   a. True
   b. False

7. After configuring the system to audit for failed logons, you purposely attempt several failed logon attempts. After logging on as Administrator, you look at the System Log and do not see any failed logon audit events. Why?
   a. You enabled the wrong policy.
   b. You must configure auditing on individual objects before events will be recorded.
   c. Audit events are recorded in the Security Log.
   d. Only Power Users can view audit events.

OBJECTIVES

7.3.2 Configure, manage, and troubleshoot account policy

ACCOUNT POLICY

UNDERSTANDING THE OBJECTIVE

The account policy has two subpolicies: password policy and account lockout policy.

WHAT YOU REALLY NEED TO KNOW

- The password policy has six policy controls that restrict how passwords are created and changed for user accounts.
- Enforce password history prevents the reuse of a password. The default is 0.
- Maximum password age prevents passwords from being used past a certain time limit. The default is 42 days.
- Minimum password age prevents changing passwords quickly to bypass the history restriction. The default is 0 days.
- Minimum password length prevents passwords shorter than a specified number of characters. The default is 0 characters.
- The Passwords must meet complexity requirements control forces passwords to be composed of at least three character types (uppercase and lowercase, numerals, and symbols), contain no part of the user account name, and be at least six characters long. The default is disabled.
- The Store password using reversible encryption for all users in the domain control forces the operating system to store passwords in a reversible encryption. Use this only if required by a specific application or network service. The default is disabled.
- The Account lockout policy has three controls that determine when an account is locked out due to repeated unsuccessful logon attempts.
- Account lockout duration determines how long a lockout remains in effect. You can set a specific number of minutes or 0 for infinite lockout. The default is 30 minutes.
- Account lockout threshold defines the number of unsuccessful logons that will result in a user account being locked out. The default is 0. This setting must be configured before the other two account lockout settings can be configured.
- The Reset account lockout counter after control defines the number of minutes the unsuccessful logon attempts count is maintained. The default is 30.
- To troubleshoot account policies, double-check all of your settings. If a locked out account fails to return to non-locked-out status, manually edit the account's properties and deselect the lockout check box. Restart the system to ensure changes take effect.
- Changes to password policy apply only to password changes and new passwords; all existing passwords are grandfathered.

OBJECTIVES ON THE JOB

Requiring strong passwords and limiting logon attempts greatly improves the security of a system.

PRACTICE TEST QUESTIONS

1. Which of the following password policies is not set to 0 or disabled by default?
   a. Enforce password history
   b. Maximum password age
   c. Minimum password length
   d. Passwords must meet complexity requirements

2. Which of the following password policies prevents reuse of passwords?
   a. Enforce password history
   b. Maximum password age
   c. Minimum password length
   d. Passwords must meet complexity requirements

3. You create a new user account and define a password of "EASYtoGUESS". Then you enable the Passwords must meet complexity requirements control of the password policy. Assuming all other settings are at their defaults, when must you change this password?
   a. Immediately
   b. In 30 minutes
   c. In 42 days
   d. In one day

4. You create a user account named egor12 for Robert Allen Smith. His e-mail address is starfire90@mycompany.com. He wants to use StarFire90Blues as the password to log on to the network. Which of the following policy settings would prevent him from using this password?
   a. Enforce password history
   b. Maximum password age
   c. Minimum password length
   d. None of the above

5. The account lockout threshold has been set to three. All other policy settings remain at their defaults. After two failed logon attempts because I mistyped my password, I realize that one more failed attempt will lock out my account. Assuming I will mistype my password at least one more time before getting it correct, which of the following actions will allow me to gain the quickest access to my desktop?
   a. Wait 30 minutes before attempting another logon.
   b. Attempt the next logon, and then wait 30 minutes for the lockout to expire.
   c. Attempt the next logon, and then wait 42 minutes for the lockout to expire.
   d. Attempt the next logon immediately, have an administrator remove the lockout on my account immediately, and then log on.

6. The password policy can be used to define a custom maximum limit for the number of characters in a password.
   a. True
   b. False

OBJECTIVES

7.3.3 Configure, manage, and troubleshoot user and group rights

USER RIGHTS

UNDERSTANDING THE OBJECTIVE

User rights control a wide range of activities on a system. While the default assignment of user rights is sufficient in most cases, some fine-tuning can result in a more secure system.

WHAT YOU REALLY NEED TO KNOW

- User rights are assigned through the user rights assignment policy of the Local Security Settings console.
- Windows XP has nearly 40 user rights.
- User rights can be assigned to individual users and/or groups.
- Managing user rights requires adding user or group names to the application list for each user right, or removing those user or group names.
- Many user rights have default assignments for specific users and groups.
- The Access this computer from the network user right can be made more secure by removing the Everyone and the Administrators groups, and adding the Authenticated Users group. This forces administrators to log on physically instead of being able to access any system over the network.
- Restore files and directories should be revoked for the Backup Operators as an additional level of security because the default allows Backup Operators to restore NTFS access-permission-protected files to FAT/FAT32 volumes.
- Bypass traverse checking should be revoked for Everyone and granted to Authenticated Users to require that non-Authenticated Users have defined access permissions at each parent folder to access a resource.
- In most cases, it is necessary to log off and log back on before changes to user rights are put into effect for the current user account.
- To troubleshoot user rights, double-check all settings to grant a user rights to users and groups.

OBJECTIVES ON THE JOB

Management of user rights is an essential part of maintaining a secure networking environment. It is a wise practice to review the assignment of user rights to ensure they are properly configured for your security needs.

PRACTICE TEST QUESTIONS

1. **User rights are managed through:**
    a. Computer Management
    b. User Accounts
    c. Local Security Settings
    d. File and Settings Transfer Wizard

2. **User rights can be assigned to:**
    a. user accounts only
    b. groups only
    c. user accounts and/or groups
    d. computer accounts

3. **Management of user rights involves:**
    a. defining Registry settings for the actions or restrictions of each user right
    b. adding users and groups from the granted list for each user right, or removing them
    c. creating programming scripts to control user activities
    d. adjusting the access permissions on system-level file objects

4. **Granting the Access this computer from the network user right to the Authenticated Users group and removing it for the Everyone and the Administrators groups creates a more secure environment.**
    a. True
    b. False

5. **Granting the Access this computer from the network user right to the Authenticated Users group and removing the user right for the Everyone and the Administrators groups creates an easy-to-manage environment.**
    a. True
    b. False

6. **If a change in the settings for user rights fails to take effect immediately after the alteration, what should you do?**
    a. Reinstall Windows XP.
    b. Restart Windows XP.
    c. Stop and restart the kernel service.
    d. Log off and log back on.

7. **Granting the Bypass traverse checking user right to the Everyone group results in a more secure environment.**
    a. True
    b. False

OBJECTIVES

7.3.4 Troubleshoot cache credentials

CACHED CREDENTIALS

UNDERSTANDING THE OBJECTIVE

Every domain account logon or .NET Passport logon is automatically cached by Windows XP. Cached credentials are used to enable a single logon by supplying the user's credentials from the cache whenever another logon is required.

WHAT YOU REALLY NEED TO KNOW

- Windows XP by default caches the last 10 logons made from the system.
- Cached logons are used to enable a single logon as well as enable system logon if the domain controller cannot be contacted.
- Caching can be disabled through Group Policy or through the Registry. The Group Policy setting is within the security options policy and is named Network access: Do not allow storage of credentials or .NET Passports for network authentication. The Registry entry is cachedlogonscount, which is located in the HKEY_LOCAL_MACHINE\SOFTWARE\ Microsoft\Windows NT\ CurrentVersion\WinLogon key. The default is 10. To disable caching, set it to 0.
- To alter the number of credentials cached, either edit the Registry and change the value of cachedlogonscount, or configure the Group Policy security option of Interactive logon: Number of previous logons to cache (in case the domain controller is not available). The default value of both of these controls is 10.
- Disabling caching is a more secure setting.
- Cached logons can be managed through Stored User Names and Passwords. This utility is accessed through the User Accounts applet. If you are a domain member, click the Advanced tab and then click Manage Passwords. If you are not a domain member, click the account name and then click Manage my network passwords from the Related Tasks list. From this window you can add, remove, or edit stored credentials.
- If you are being authenticated with the wrong user account or to the wrong access level, you should edit or remove the cached credential for that site.
- If you cannot access resources that you should have access to or previously could access, you may have an expired account or password. Edit the cached credential for that site.
- If you can access a resource or system that you should not be authorized to access, you may have a cached credential from another account. Remove the cached credential for that site. You may also consider disabling credential caching altogether.

OBJECTIVES ON THE JOB

Cached credentials support a less-annoying single logon feature, but single logons can become a security problem, especially if multiple users log on using the same client or if the client is ever stolen.

PRACTICE TEST QUESTIONS

1. Windows XP caches the logon credentials for the last _____ user(s), by default.
   a. one
   b. two
   c. five
   d. 10

2. Cached credentials provide what benefit? (Choose all that apply.)
   a. Automatic logon upon startup
   b. Single logon for multiple network services
   c. Easy access to other users' logon credentials
   d. Access to desktop and network when domain controller is unavailable

3. Cached logons can be disabled using which of the following methods? (Choose all that apply.)
   a. Editing the Registry
   b. Configuring the User Accounts applet
   c. Altering the Group Policy
   d. Booting into the Recovery console

4. Allowing cached credentials to be stored by Windows XP is a more secure configuration.
   a. True
   b. False

5. Existing cached credentials can be edited and deleted.
   a. True
   b. False

6. If your logon credentials for a site have expired, you should:
   a. delete the cached credentials
   b. disable cached credentials
   c. edit the cached credentials
   d. set the number of cached credentials to five

7. If you are automatically logged on to a site with another user account's credentials, you should: (Choose all that apply.)
   a. consider disabling cached credentials
   b. reinstall Windows XP
   c. delete the cached credentials
   d. set the number of cached credentials to 20

OBJECTIVES

7.4 Configure, manage, and troubleshoot a security configuration

SECURITY CONFIGURATION • SECEDIT

UNDERSTANDING THE OBJECTIVE

Secedit is used to configure security on systems. With Secedit, you can quickly configure the security on a large number of systems using a single command rather than manually configuring each setting on each system.

WHAT YOU REALLY NEED TO KNOW

- Secedit is the command-line version of the Security Configuration and Analysis Tool. Secedit can be used to analyze, configure, export, and validate security on a system.
- Secedit functions through the use of templates, preconfigured group policies, and file access permission sets used to compare or configure a system's security.
- Windows XP includes seven predefined security templates. However, two of them are for domain controller use only. The others are: compatws (security is configured to the most compatible with nonsecured applications); hisecws (security is configured as high as possible); rootsec (applies default root permissions to the boot partition); securews (security is configured at a moderate level); and setup security (security is reset to just-installed defaults).
- The four functions of Secedit are controlled through primary parameters: /analyze, /configure, /export, and /validate. Each primary parameter has numerous subparameters. The analyze function compares the current security of a system with a security template and produces a report of any differences. The configure function applies a security template to a system. The export function creates a security template from the security configuration of a system. The validate function is used to check the syntax of a security template before it is applied to a system.
- If a system fails to meet security requirements, use Secedit to apply a security template.
- Troubleshooting security configuration generally involves performing an analysis with Secedit against the security template with which the system should comply. Reported differences should be corrected manually, or you can perform a configure operation to apply the security template to the system.
- If Secedit fails to function, make sure you are logged on as Administrator, verify that no applications are running, and consider restarting the system. You should also check the current security template for problems; a corrupt security template does not work at all or enters invalid or incorrect configurations on the destination system when applied.

OBJECTIVES ON THE JOB

Secedit is a great timesaver, but it is important that you understand the contents of each security template used to configure your systems. It is a good practice to create your own security templates instead of relying on those provided by Microsoft.

PRACTICE TEST QUESTIONS

1. To check the syntax of a security template, you should issue what command?
   a. secedit /configure
   b. secedit /validate
   c. secedit /analyze
   d. secedit /export

2. To apply a security template to a system, you should issue what command?
   a. secedit /configure
   b. secedit /validate
   c. secedit /analyze
   d. secedit /export

3. To check a system for compliance with a security template, you should issue what command?
   a. secedit /configure
   b. secedit /validate
   c. secedit /analyze
   d. secedit /export

4. If a security template does not offer the exact level of security you need for your systems, what should you do?
   a. Apply the highest-level security template available and manually disable unnecessary configurations.
   b. Configure a system to your exact specifications, and then create a security template from that system to apply to all other systems.
   c. Use one of the predefined security templates and adjust it to your company's needs.
   d. Apply the lowest-level security template available and manually enable all necessary additional configurations.

5. After applying a security template to a system, you perform several checks to test the security. You discover that some restrictions are in place and working properly while others are either not in place, not taking effect, or are completely incorrect. What should you do?
   a. Apply another security template.
   b. Apply the same security template again.
   c. Validate the current security template.
   d. Manually reconfigure this and all other systems to which this security template was applied.

6. You are required to perform a security audit every year. In the past, you've performed this audit by manually checking nearly 240 settings on each system. What other method simplifies this process, yet increases the accuracy?
   a. Create a security template from each system.
   b. Perform a validation scan on all systems with Secedit.
   c. Apply the hisecws security template to all systems.
   d. Perform an analysis scan on all systems with Secedit.

OBJECTIVES

7.5 Configure, manage, and troubleshoot Internet Explorer security settings

IE SECURITY SETTINGS

UNDERSTANDING THE OBJECTIVE

Internet Explorer security settings are controlled primarily through the Internet Options applet's Security tab. On this tab you can define and manage security zones.

WHAT YOU REALLY NEED TO KNOW

- A security zone is an area of cyberspace with a predefined level of security restrictions, which are applied to all resources assigned to that zone. The zones defined on the Security tab are Internet, Local intranet, Trusted sites, and Restricted sites.
- You can assign one of four predefined security levels to each zone, or customize the security for each zone.
- The Low level provides only minimal safeguards and warnings. Most content is downloaded and run without prompts, and all active content can run. This is the default security level for the Trusted sites zone.
- The Medium-low level provides the same safeguards as Medium but without prompts. Most content is run without prompts, and unsigned ActiveX controls cannot be downloaded. This is the default security level for the Local intranet zone.
- The Medium level provides safe browsing while retaining functionality, prompts before downloading potentially unsafe content, and does not allow unsigned ActiveX controls to be downloaded. This is the default security level for the Internet zone.
- The High level provides safe browsing with the least functionality, all less-secure features are disabled, and no unsigned or potentially unsafe content can be downloaded. This is the default security level for the Restricted sites zone.
- The Internet zone contains all sites not assigned to one of the other three zones. The Local intranet zone contains all sites within your local network. This list is a combination of all local sites not listed in the Trusted sites or Restricted sites zones, all sites accessed by bypassing the proxy server, and all network UNC paths. Trusted sites and Restricted sites contain only those sites you manually add (via the Sites button). Place only those sites that you fully trust in the Trusted sites zone.
- If you cannot access a site fully, or if you can access most of a site that should be restricted, verify the following: the definition of the site within one of the zones is correct, the site is not repeated in more than one zone, and the security settings of that zone are correct.

OBJECTIVES ON THE JOB

The security zones of IE offer a reasonable level of security if you are vigilant about adding sites to the Trusted sites and Restricted sites zones. However, until you define a site as a Restricted sites zone member, it is still a member of the Internet zone, which has only medium-level security.

PRACTICE TEST QUESTIONS

1. **The Medium level of security for security zones corresponds to which of the following security definitions?**
    a. Provides safe browsing with the least functionality, all less-secure features are disabled, and no unsigned or potentially unsafe content is downloaded.
    b. Provides the same safeguards but without prompts, most content will be run without prompts, and unsigned ActiveX controls will not be downloaded.
    c. Provides only minimal safeguards and warnings, most content is downloaded and run without prompts, and all active content can run.
    d. Provides safe browsing while retaining functionality, prompts before downloading potentially unsafe content, and unsigned ActiveX controls will not be downloaded.

2. **What is the default security level of the Internet zone?**
    a. Low
    b. Medium-low
    c. Medium
    d. High

3. **What is the default security level of the Local intranet zone?**
    a. Low
    b. Medium-low
    c. Medium
    d. High

4. **What site is a member of the Local intranet zone? (Choose all that apply.)**
    a. All sites not defined as members of the Trusted sites and Restricted sites zones
    b. All sites using https:// as a prefix
    c. All UNC network paths
    d. All sites accessed by bypassing the proxy server

5. **How are sites added to the Trusted sites and Restricted sites zones?**
    a. Press the Add-to-Zone button on the toolbar while surfing
    b. Edit the zone value entry in the Registry
    c. Automatically, based on the results of a scan by IE
    d. Manually entered on the Security tab through the Sites button

6. **If you can access features of a site that should be restricted from use, what action should you take to resolve this? (Choose all that apply.)**
    a. Reset all zones to have a security of High.
    b. Double-check the site's definition within a zone.
    c. Verify that the site is listed as a member of a single zone only.
    d. Check that you are not logged on as Administrator.

7. **The *http://blue.mycompany.com/* Web site is testing new ActiveX controls and downloadable components. This site is located within your company's network. You've been asked to test this site. The zone is located in which site by default?**
    a. Internet
    b. Local intranet
    c. Trusted sites

GLOSSARY OF ACRONYMS AND ABBREVIATIONS

A
ACPI – Advanced Configuration Power Interface
APM – Advanced Power Management

B
BIOS – Basic Input/Output System

C
CD-R – Compact Disk-Recordable
CD-ROM – Compact Disk Read-Only Memory
CD-RW – Compact Disk-Rewritable
CPU – Central Processing Unit
CSID – Called Station Identification

D
DHCP – Dynamic Host Configuration Protocol
DNS – Domain Name System
DPI – dots per inch
DPMI – DOS Protected Mode Interface
DVD – Digital Video Disk

E
EFS – Encrypting File System

F
FAT – File Allocation Table
FTP – File Transfer Protocol

G
GUI – graphical user interface

H
HCL – Hardware Compatibility List
HTTP – Hypertext Transfer Protocol
HTTPS – Hypertext Transfer Protocol Secure Sockets

I
I/O – Input/Output
ICF – Internet Connection Firewall
ICMP – Internet Control Message Protocol
ICS – Internet Sharing Connection
IE – Internet Explorer
IIS – Internet Information Server
IKE – Internet Key Exchange
IMAP3 – Internet Message Access Protocol 3
IP – Internet Protocol
IPP – Internet Printing Protocol
IR – infrared
IrDA – Infrared Data Association
IRQ – Interrupt Request
ISA – Industry Standard Architecture
ISP – Internet service provider

L
L2TP – Layer 2 Tunneling Protocol
LAN – local area network
LCD – Liquid Crystal Display
LCP – Local Computer Policy
LKGC – Last Known Good Configuration

M
MMC – Microsoft Management Console
MSN – Microsoft Network

N
NetBIOS – Network Basic Input/Output System
NIC – network interface card
NTFS – NT File System

O
OU – Organizational Unit

P

PCI – Peripheral Component Interconnect
POP3 – Post Office Protocol 3
PPP – Point-to-Point Protocol
PPTP – Point-to-Point Tunneling Protocol
PXE – Pre-Boot Execution Environment

R

RAID – Redundant Array of Inexpensive Disks
RAM – Random Access Memory
RIS – Remote Installation Services

S

SAM – Sequential Access Method
SLIP – Serial Line Internet Protocol
SMTP – Simple Mail Transfer Protocol
SVGA – Super Video Graphics Adapter
SYSPREP – System Preparation Tool

T

TCP/IP – Transmission Control Protocol/Internet Protocol
TSID – Transmitting Station Identification

U

UDF – uniqueness database file
UDP – User Datagram Protocol
UNC – Universal Naming Convention
UPS – Universal Power Supply
URL – Uniform Resource Locator
USB – Universal Serial Bus

V

VM – virtual machine
VPN – virtual private network

W

WINS – Windows Internet Naming Service

ANSWER KEY

Section 1.0
Objective 1.1
Practice Questions:
1. b
2. a, b, d, f
3. b
4. a
5. c
6. b
7. b

Objective 1.2
Practice Questions:
1. a, b, d
2. a
3. b
4. a, b
5. b
6. a
7. b

Objective 1.2.1
Practice Questions:
1. b
2. a, c, d
3. c
4. a
5. c
6. b

Objective 1.2.2
Practice Questions:
1. b
2. c
3. a, b, d
4. d
5. b, c
6. b, c
7. a

Objective 1.2.3
Practice Questions:
1. a, b, d
2. b
3. a, c
4. a, d
5. a, c, e, f, g
6. a
7. a, c, e

Objective 1.3
Practice Questions:
1. b
2. b
3. b, c
4. b
5. a
6. b
7. b

Objective 1.3.1
Practice Questions:
1. a
2. b
3. b
4. b
5. a
6. a, b
7. a

Objective 1.3.2
Practice Questions:
1. a, c, d
2. c
3. b
4. b
5. b
6. b
7. a

Objective 1.4
Practice Questions:
1. c
2. c
3. a, d
4. c
5. b
6. b
7. b

Objective 1.5
Practice Questions:
1. b
2. c
3. d
4. b
5. c
6. a
7. b

Section 2.0
Objective 2.1
Practice Questions:
1. a, c
2. b, c
3. a
4. a, b, c, d
5. b, d
6. b
7. b

Objective 2.1.1
Practice Questions:
1. a, b, d
2. b
3. a
4. c
5. a, b, d, e, g, h
6. a, c
7. a, d

Objective 2.1.2
Practice Questions:
1. b
2. a
3. b
4. c
5. d
6. a
7. a

Objective 2.1.3
Practice Questions:
1. a
2. a, b, c, d
3. a
4. b, e
5. c, d
6. a
7. a

Objective 2.2
Practice Questions:
1. a, b, d
2. b
3. c
4. b
5. a
6. b
7. a, c

Objective 2.2.1
Practice Questions:
1. a
2. b
3. c
4. c
5. c
6. a
7. d

Objective 2.3
Practice Questions:
1. b
2. a, c, d
3. a
4. a, c, d
5. a
6. c
7. a, b, d, e

Objective 2.3.1
Practice Questions:
1. b
2. a, c, d
3. b
4. a
5. b
6. a
7. d

Objective 2.3.2
Practice Questions:
1. a, b, c
2. a, c
3. b, c
4. b
5. a, b, d
6. b, c, d
7. b

Objective 2.3.3
Practice Questions:
1. d
2. b, c
3. a, b, d
4. b
5. b
6. b
7. b

Objective 2.4
Practice Questions:
1. a, c
2. b
3. a, c
4. c
5. b, d
6. b, c
7. a, b, d

Objective 2.5
Practice Questions:
1. c
2. b
3. a
4. a
5. a
6. c, d
7. a, b, d, f

Objective 2.6
Practice Questions:
1. b
2. b
3. b
4. a, b, d, e
5. a, c, d
6. a, b, d
7. b

Section 3.0
Objective 3.1
Practice Questions:
1. b
2. b
3. d
4. b
5. b
6. d
7. c

Objective 3.1.1
Practice Questions:
1. a, c, d
2. a, b, d
3. b
4. b
5. d
6. b
7. a, b, d, f

Objective 3.1.2
Practice Questions:
1. b
2. c, e, g
3. a
4. c
5. a
6. a, c, d, f, g, i

Objective 3.2
Practice Questions:
1. a, d
2. a, c, d, f
3. c
4. c
5. c
6. a

Objective 3.2.1
Practice Questions:
1. d
2. c
3. b
4. b
5. b
6. a, e
7. a

Objective 3.3
Practice Questions:
1. b
2. c, d
3. a, c
4. b
5. a
6. a
7. a

Objective 3.4.1
Practice Questions:
1. b
2. a, c, d
3. a, b, d
4. b, c (Computer Management hosts the Device Manager as a subset tool)
5. b
6. a, b, d, e
7. a

Objective 3.4.2
Practice Questions:
1. a, b, d
2. a, b
3. a, b, d
4. b
5. b
6. b

Objective 3.5
Practice Questions:
1. b
2. a
3. b
4. c
5. c
6. b
7. b (the Sigverif.txt file will not contain data about files it did not scan)

Objective 3.6
Practice Questions:
1. b
2. c
3. b
4. b
5. b
6. b
7. b

Section 4.0
Objective 4.1
Practice Questions:
1. c
2. a
3. a, b, c
4. b
5. b
6. a, b, d
7. a

Objective 4.1.1
Practice Questions:
1. c
2. a, b
3. a
4. d
5. b, c
6. a
7. c

Objective 4.1.2
Practice Questions:
1. b
2. b
3. a
4. c
5. b
6. a, b, d
7. b

Objective 4.1.3
Practice Questions:
1. b
2. a
3. d
4. c
5. b
6. a
7. a, d

Objective 4.1.4
Practice Questions:
1. a
2. a
3. a
4. b
5. d
6. b
7. c

Objective 4.1.5
Practice Questions:
1. a, b, d
2. b
3. a, b, c
4. c, d
5. d
6. a
7. b

Objective 4.2
Practice Questions:
1. c
2. c
3. a, c
4. d
5. b, c
6. a

Objective 4.3
Practice Questions:
1. c
2. c
3. c
4. b
5. b
6. a

Objective 4.3.1
Practice Questions:
1. 1-a, b; 2-a, d; 3-a, b, d, e; 4-d, e; 5-c; 6-e
2. a, b
3. d
4. c

Objective 4.3.2
Practice Questions:
1. b, c
2. b
3. a, b, d, e, f
4. a
5. b
6. b

Objective 4.3.3
Practice Questions:
1. a, c, e, g
2. b, d
3. b, c, e, h
4. b
5. c
6. b
7. b

Section 5.0
Objective 5.1
Practice Questions:
1. a
2. d
3. b
4. a
5. b, d
6. b
7. b

Objective 5.2
Practice Questions:
1. b, c
2. b
3. b
4. b
5. d
6. c

Objective 5.3
Practice Questions:
1. a, b, d
2. a, c, d
3. b
4. a, c, d
5. a
6. b
7. a

Objective 5.4
Practice Questions:
1. c
2. b
3. d
4. a, c, d
5. a
6. b
7. a

Objective 5.5
  Practice Questions:
  1. a
  2. 1-b, 2-d, 3-a, 4-e, 5-c
  3. b
  4. b
  5. a
  6. c
  7. a

Section 6.0
Objective 6.1
  Practice Questions:
  1. b
  2. a, b, c
  3. a
  4. c, d
  5. c
  6. c
  7. a

Objective 6.2
  Practice Questions:
  1. b
  2. b
  3. a, c, d
  4. d
  5. b, e, g
  6. a, b, c, d, e, f, or just f

Objective 6.3
  Practice Questions:
  1. b
  2. b
  3. b
  4. a, b, c
  5. b, c, d
  6. a
  7. a

Objective 6.4
Practice Questions:
1. b
2. a, c
3. b
4. b
5. b
6. d
7. b

Objective 6.5
Practice Questions:
1. a
2. a
3. b
4. a
5. a, b, d
6. a, c, d
7. a

Objective 6.6
Practice Questions:
1. c
2. c, d
3. c
4. c
5. a
6. a, b, c, d

Section 7.0
Objective 7.1
Practice Questions:
1. a
2. b
3. c, d
4. d
5. b
6. b
7. a

Objective 7.2
Practice Questions:
1. b
2. b
3. c
4. d
5. a, c, d, g, h, j, k
6. a

Objective 7.3
Practice Questions:
1. b
2. a, d
3. a, b, c, d
4. b
5. a
6. b, d
7. b, d

Objective 7.3.1
Practice Questions:
1. b
2. c
3. b
4. c, d
5. d
6. a
7. c

Objective 7.3.2
Practice Questions:
1. b
2. a
3. c
4. d
5. d
6. b

Objective 7.3.3
Practice Questions:
1. c
2. c
3. b
4. a
5. b
6. d
7. b

Objective 7.3.4
Practice Questions:
1. d
2. b, d
3. a, c
4. b
5. a
6. c
7. a, c

Objective 7.4
Practice Questions:
1. b
2. a
3. c
4. b
5. c
6. d

Objective 7.5
Practice Questions:
1. d
2. c
3. b
4. a, c, d
5. d
6. b, c
7. b

INDEX

A

access. *See also* permissions
　denying, 28, 32, 40, 56
　management, 24–25
　optimizing, 30–31
　to printers, 40–41
　troubleshooting, 24–25,
　　32–33, 46–47
Accessibility applet, 106–107
accessibility services, 106–107
Accessibility Wizard, 106
account(s)
　lockout, 132–133
　policies, 132–133
　settings, administering,
　　128–129
ACPI (Advanced
　Configuration Power
　Interface), 62–63, 86, 87
Activate Windows tool, 18
activation, 18–19
ActiveX controls (Microsoft),
　140–141
Add Hardware applet,
　64, 66–67
Add Printer Wizard, 36
Add Scheduled Task
　Wizard, 84
Administrators group, 94,
　128, 131
Advanced Configuration
　Power Interface (ACPI),
　62–63, 86, 87
answer files, 10–11
APM (Advanced Power
　Management), 62
Appearance tab, 58
applets
　Accessibility applet,
　　106–107
　Add Hardware applet,
　　64, 66–67

Display applet, 58,
　60–61, 104
Dualview applet, 60–61
Folder Options applet,
　26, 46
Internet Options applet, 140
Language Options
　applet, 100
Phone and Modem Options
　applet, 64, 100
Power Options applet, 62
Regional and Language
　Options applet, 100–101
Scanners and Cameras
　applet, 64–65
System applet, 18, 82, 118
User Accounts applet, 128
application(s)
　managing, with Windows
　　Installer, 102–103
　optimizing, 82–83
　troubleshooting, 82–83
Application log, 82
Applications tab, 74
Authenticated Users group,
　134, 135
AUTOEXEC.BAT, 82–83
AUTOEXEC.NET, 82
Automatic Updates tab, 18
AutoPlay, 54, 55

B

back up operations, 88–95
Backup Operators group,
　128, 134
bad sectors, 44
Basic Input Output System
　(BIOS), 62
battery power, 86
Battery Status object, 86
bindings, 30
BIOS (Basic Input Output
　System), 62

bookmarks, 114
browsers. *See* Internet
　Explorer browser

C

cached credentials, 136–137
caching, 30–31, 46. *See also*
　cached credentials
　adding more, 76
　disk device management
　　and, 52
　processor optimization and,
　　78–79
cameras, digital, 64–67
CD-ROM devices, 2–3, 54–55
Change permission, 32–33, 40
Cleaner Management
　Wizard, 56
cloning systems, 8–9
Close Open File command, 24
Computer Management tool,
　24–25, 52–53, 56
CONFIG.NT, 82–83
CONFIG.SYS, 82
Control Panel
　Accessibility applet,
　　106–107
　Add Hardware applet,
　　64, 66–67
　Display applet, 58,
　　60–61, 104
　Dualview applet, 60–61
　Folder Options applet,
　　26, 46
　Internet Options applet, 140
　Language Options
　　applet, 100
　Phone and Modem Options
　　applet, 64, 100
　Power Options applet, 62
　Regional and Language
　　Options applet, 100–101
　Scanners and Cameras
　　applet, 64–65

System applet, 18, 82, 118
User Accounts applet, 128
Control permission, 56, 57
CONVERT utility, 44–45
CPUs (central processing units), 2–3, 14, 70–71, 78–79
CSIDs, 48

D

debugging, 92. *See also* errors
Debugging Mode option, 92
defragmentation, 44–45, 52–53
Deny setting, 28, 32
desktop. *See also* Remote Desktop
  environment, configuring, 97–107
  remote, 112, 118–120
  troubleshooting, 74–75, 104–105, 118–119
Device Manager, 64–65, 70
DHCP (Dynamic Host Configuration Protocol), 6–7, 110, 113
dial-up networking, 112–113
digital cameras, 64–67
Directory Services Restore Mode option, 92
DirectX applications, 58
disk(s)
  cleanup, 44–45, 52–53
  defragmenting, 44–45, 52–53
  devices, managing, 52–53
  performance, optimizing/troubleshooting, 80–81
Disk Management tool, 52–53
Display applet, 58, 60–61, 104
display devices, 58–61, 64–67, 92, 104
Documents and Settings folder, 98
DOS (Disk Operating System), 82, 83

DPMI (DOS Protected Mode Interface), 82
Driver Signing Options dialog box, 68
drivers
  managing/troubleshooting, 68–69
  signing, 68–69
Dualview applet, 60–61
DVD devices, 2–3, 14, 54–55

E

EFS (Encrypting File System), 124–125
e-mail utilities, 118
Enable Boot logging option, 92
Enable VGA Mode option, 92
encryption, 26, 27
  EFS, 124-125
  mobile use and, 86
  offline files and, 46
error(s). *See also* debugging
  checking, 44–45, 52–53
  media, 20
  syntax, 11
Event Viewer, 20, 82–83, 130

F

Fastwiz.exe, 16
FAT file system, 52, 134
  configuring, 44–45
  converting to, 44–45
  file compression and, 26, 27
FAT32 file system, 44–45, 52, 134
Fax Console, 48–49
fax modems, 48
Fax Monitor, 48
Fax Security tab, 48
file systems. *See also* NTFS (Windows NT File System)
  configuring, 44–45
  converting, 44–45
  FAT, 26, 27, 44–45, 52, 134

FAT32, 44–45, 52, 134
  managing, 44–45
File Transfer Protocol (FTP), 112, 114–117, 120–121
files. *See also* file systems
  access to, administering, 24–25, 28–31
  answer, 10–11
  compression of, administering, 26–27
  log, 68–69, 74, 84–85
  offline, 30, 46–47, 86
  orphaned, 44
  synchronization of, 46–47
Files and Settings Transfer Wizard, 16, 17
FilterKeys, 106–107
firewalls, 120–121
Folder Options applet, 26, 46
folders
  access to, administering, 24–25, 28–33
  shared, 24, 25, 32–33
Foreign Disk command, 52
FTP (File Transfer Protocol), 112, 114–117, 120–121
Full Control permission, 28, 29, 32–33, 40–41

G

group(s)
  administering, 128–129
  permissions and, 28–29, 134–135
  policies, 102
  shared folders and, 32, 33
Guest account, 98
Guests group, 128
GUIs (graphical user interfaces), 2, 90, 92–93

H

hard disk(s)
  cleanup, 44–45, 52–53

defragmenting, 44–45, 52–53
devices, managing, 52–53
performance, optimizing/troubleshooting, 80–81
HCL (Hardware Compatibility List), 2, 14, 20, 66
HIMEM.SYS, 82
History list, 114, 115
HTTP (HyperText Transfer Protocol), 112, 114, 120
HTTPS (HyperText Transfer Protocol, Secure Sockets), 112, 114

I

ICF (Internet Connection Firewall), 120–121
ICMP (Internet Control Message Protocol), 120
ICMP tab, 120
ICS (Internet Connection Sharing), 112–113
IIS (Microsoft Internet Information Services), 34–35, 42, 116–118, 121
IKE (Internet Key Exchange), 112
IMAP3 (Internet Message Access Protocol 3), 112, 120
IMAP4 (Internet Message Access Protocol 4), 112, 120
input/output (I/O) devices, 64–67
installation
  of CD-ROM devices, 54–55
  of DVD devices, 54–55
  failed, troubleshooting, 20–21
  migrating existing user environments and, 16–17
  performing updates after, 18–19
  product activation after, 18–19
  Windows XP Professional, 2–20
InstallShield, 102
Internet Connection Firewall (ICF), 120–121
Internet Connection Sharing (ICS), 112–113
Internet Explorer browser, 18, 114–115, 140–141
Internet Options applet, 140
Internet Protocol (IP), 4, 5, 110, 113, 116
IrDA (Infrared Data Association) devices, 64–67
IRQs (Interrupt Requests), 66
ISA (Industry Standard Architecture), 62

K

keyboards, troubleshooting/managing, 64–67

L

L2TP (Layer 2 Tunneling Protocol), 112, 113
Language Options applet, 100
languages, multiple, 100–101
Languages tab, 100
LANs (local area networks), 14, 86
LE, 102
List Folder Content permission, 28
LKGC (Last Know Good Configuration), 88, 89, 92, 104–105
LMHOSTS, 110
local security policy, 126–127
Local Users and Groups tool, 128
log files, 68–69, 74, 84–85
LogicalDisk object counters, 52

M

Magnifier, 106
Manage Documents permission, 40–41, 42
Manage Printers permission, 40–41, 42
MAPI, 118
memory. *See also* RAM (Random Access Memory)
  access optimization and, 30–31
  application optimization and, 82
  file compression and, 26
  optimization, 76–77
  troubleshooting, 76–77
mobile users, optimization of, 86–87
modems, troubleshooting/managing, 64–67
Modify permission, 28, 56
monitors, 58–61, 64–67
mouse. *See* input/output (I/O) devices
multiple
  displays, configuring support for, 60–61
  language support, 100–101
multiprocessors, 70–71, 78–79. *See also* processors

N

Narrator, 106
.NET Passports, 136
NetBIOS names, 110
NetBIOS over TCP/IP, 110
Network Configuration Operators group, 128, 129
NICs (network interface cards), 2, 20, 86, 110–111
Normal Mode, 58
NTBTLOG.TXT, 92
NTCONFIG.POL, 126–127

NTFS (Windows NT File System). *See also* file systems
  access optimization and, 30
  configuring, 44–45
  converting from, 44–45
  disk device management and, 52
  file compression and, 26, 27
  IIS and, 116
  permissions and, 34, 40, 134
  printers and, 40
  shared folders and, 32, 33
  user rights and, 134
  Web resource management and, 34–35
NTUSER.DAT, 98, 99
NTUSER.MAN, 98, 99
NTVDM, 82, 83

O

Offline Files utility, 30, 46–47, 86
Open Files subnode, 24, 25
optimization. *See also* performance
  of access to files and folders, 30–31
  of applications, 82–83
  of disk performance, 80–81
  of memory, 76–77
  of mobile users, 86–87
  of processor, 78–79
orphaned files, 44
Outlook Express (Microsoft), 118

P

page faults, 76–77
passwords, 34, 87, 132–133, 136
PCI (Peripheral Connect Interface), 80
performance. *See also* optimization
  auditing and, 130
  processors and, 70–71, 74
  removable media and, 56–57
  video adapters and, 58–59
Performance Options dialog box, 58, 74, 82
Performance tab, 70, 74
permissions. *See also* access; security
  basic description of, 28–29
  printers and, 40–41
  problems with, 24
  removable media and, 56
  shared folders and, 32–33
  Web resource management and, 34–35
Phone and Modem Options applet, 64, 100
PhysicalDisk object counters, 52
PING, 111, 120
Plug and Play, 54, 58
Point-to-Point Protocol (PPP), 112
POP3 (Post Office Protocol, Version 3), 112, 120
power management, 62–63, 86
Power Options applet, 62
Power Users group, 128
PPTP (Point-to-Point Tunneling Protocol), 112
Print permission, 40
printers
  answer files and, 10
  controlling access to, 40–41
  connecting to, 36–37, 42–43
  fax support and, 48
  Internet, 42–43
  managing, 38–39
  permissions for, 40–41
  troubleshooting/managing, 64–67

Printers and Faxes utility, 36–37, 48
Processes tab, 70, 74, 82
Processor object, 70
processors, 2–3, 14
  multi-, 70–71, 78–79
  optimizing, 78–79
  troubleshooting, 78–79
product activation, 18–19
Properties dialog box, 26, 32, 39, 54, 89
  fax support and, 48
  IIS and, 116
  I/O devices and, 66

R

RAID (Redundant Array of Inexpensive Disks), 80
RAM (Random Access Memory), 2–3, 62. *See also* memory
  disk optimization and, 80–81
  optimization, 76–77
  saving the system state to, 86
  shortages, 76, 77, 80
  system requirements and, 14
Read & Execute permission, 28, 29
Read permission, 28, 29, 32–33, 40
Recovery Console, 88, 94–95
Recycle Bin, 104–105
Regional and Language Options applet, 100–101
Regional Options tab, 100
Registry, 84, 88, 94, 136
Remote Assistance, 118–119
Remote Desktop, 112, 118–120. *See also* desktop
Remote Desktop Connection utility, 118

Remote Desktop Users group, 128
Remote Installation Services (RIS), 6–7, 10
Removable Storage, 56–57
removal media, monitoring/configuring, 56–57
Replicator group, 128
restore operations, 88–95
RIS (Remote Installation Services), 6–7, 10

S

Safe Mode, 58, 92–94
Safe Mode option, 92
Safe Mode with Command Prompt option, 92, 93
Safe Mode with Networking option, 92, 93
SAM database, 124
scanners, 64–65
Scanners and Cameras applet, 64–65
Scheduled Tasks utility, 84–85
Secedit (Security Configuration and Analysis Tool), 138–139
security. See also access; permissions
   for accounts, 128–132
   administering, 123–141
   auditing, 130–131
   cached credentials and, 136–137
   configurations, 138–141
   encryption and, 26, 27, 46, 86, 124–125
   fax support and, 48
   file compression and, 26, 27
   firewalls and, 120–121
   Internet Explorer settings for, 140–141
   logs, 120, 130
   mobile use and, 86
   offline files and, 46
   passwords, 34, 87, 132–133, 136
   policy, 126–127, 140–141
   Recovery Console and, 94
   zones, 140–141
Security tab, 48
Serial Line Internet Protocol (SLIP), 112
sessions, terminating, 24, 25
Setup Manager, 10–11
Setup Wizard, 12
Shared Documents folder, 32
Shared Folders, 24, 25, 32–33
Sharing tab, 30
ShowSounds, 106–107
Signature Verification tool, 68–69
Simple File Sharing, 32–33
SLIP (Serial Line Internet Protocol), 112
smart card readers. See input/output (I/O) devices
SMTP (Simple Mail Transfer Protocol), 112, 120
SoundSentry, 106–107
Special permission, 28, 40
StickyKeys, 106–107
synchronization, of files, 46–47
Synchronize Files command, 46
SYSPREP (System Preparation Tool), 8–9
system
   back up operations, 88–89
   cloning, 8–9
   duplication, 8
   files, default destination of, 2, 3
   performance, for mobile users, 86–87
   requirements, for Windows XP Professional, 2–3, 14–15
   restoration, 88–95, 102
   state data, 86, 88–95
System applet, 18, 82, 118
System Monitor, 52–53, 70, 74, 86
System Preparation Tool (SYSPREP), 8–9
System Restore, 102

T

Take Ownership permissions, 40
tape devices. See removable media
Task Manager, 70, 82
TCP (Transmission Control Protocol), 120
TCP/IP (Transmission Control Protocol/Internet Protocol), 36, 110–112
Telnet, 112, 120
Telnet Server, 120
Terminal Services, 102
ToggleKeys, 106–107
troubleshooting
   accessibility services, 106–107
   account policies, 132
   applications, 82–83
   auditing, 130–131
   desktops, 74–75, 104–105, 118–119
   disk performance, 52–53, 80–81
   drivers, 68–69
   failed installation, 20–21
   fax support, 48–49
   file access, 24–25, 32–33
   file compression, 26–27, 46–47
   file systems, 124–125
   file synchronization, 46–47
   firewalls, 120–121

folder access, 24–25, 32–33
Internet Connection Sharing, 112–113
memory, 76–77
processors, 78–79
security configurations, 138–139
security policies, 126–127
system restoration, 92–93
user and group rights, 134–135
video adapters, 58–59
Web server resources, 34–35
TSID, 48

U

UDF (uniqueness database file), 4–5
UDP (User Datagram Protocol), 112, 120
UNC paths, 140
updates, 18–19
upgrades, 12–15
URLs (Uniform Resource Locators)
  Internet Explorer and, 114
  for Internet printers, 36, 42, 43
USB (Universal Serial Bus), 36, 64–67
Use permission, 56, 57
user(s)
  administering, 128–129
  data, backing up/restoring, 88–95
  environments, migrating, 16–17
  profiles, roaming, 16, 98–99
  rights, 134–135
User Accounts applet, 128
Users group, 130
Utility Manager, 106

V

VERITAS, 102
video adapters, 58–59
viruses, 68
Visual Effects tab, 74
VMs (virtual machines), 82
volumes
  assigning drive letters to, 52
  disk device management and, 52
  scanning, for bad sectors, 44
  troubleshooting, 53–54
VPNs (virtual private networks), 31, 112–113

W

Web resource management, 34–35
Windows 2000 Server (Microsoft), 6–7, 12
Windows Backup (Microsoft), 90–91
Windows Installer (Microsoft), 102–103
Windows Media Player (Microsoft), 114
Windows Messenger Service (Microsoft), 118, 119
Windows Movie Maker (Microsoft), 14–15
Windows .NET Server (Microsoft), 6–7, 10
Windows NT File System (Microsoft). *See also* file systems
  access optimization and, 30
  configuring, 44–45
  converting from, 44–45
  disk device management and, 52
  file compression and, 26, 27
  IIS and, 116
  permissions and, 34, 40, 134
  printers and, 40
  shared folders and, 32, 33
  user rights and, 134
  Web resource management and, 34–35
Windows Update (Microsoft), 18
Windows XP Professional (Microsoft)
  desktop management, 74–75
  installation, 2–20
  migrating user environments to, 16–17
  multiple-location configurations for, 100–101
  RIS installation of, 6–7
  SYSPREP installation of, 8–9
  unattended installation of, 4–5
  upgrading to, 12–15
WINNT, 2–3, 4–5, 12
WINNT32, 2–3, 12
WINS servers, 110
wireless devices. *See* input/output (I/O) devices
Wise Solutions, 102
WOWEXEC, 82
Write permission, 28, 29

Z

.zip files, 26
zones, security, 140–141